Consumer Research
for Museum
Marketers

Consumer Research for Museum Marketers

Audience Insights Money Can't Buy

MARGOT A. WALLACE

ALTAMIRA
PRESS

A Division of
ROWMAN & LITTLEFIELD PUBLISHERS, INC.
Lanham • New York • Toronto • Plymouth, UK

Published by AltaMira Press
A division of Rowman & Littlefield Publishers, Inc.
A wholly owned subsidary of The Rowman & Littlefield Publishing Group, Inc.
4501 Forbes Boulevard, Suite 200, Lanham, Maryland 20706
http://www.altamirapress.com

Estover Road, Plymouth PL6 7PY, United Kingdom

British Library Cataloguing in Publication Information Available

Library of Congress Cataloging-in-Publication Data

Wallace, Margot A., 1941–
  Consumer research for museum marketers : audience insights money can't buy
/ Margot A. Wallace.
      p. cm.
  Includes bibliographical references and index.
  ISBN 978-0-7591-1808-9 (cloth : alk. paper) — ISBN 978-0-7591-1809-6 (pbk.
: alk. paper) — ISBN 978-0-7591-1810-2 (electronic)
  1. Museums—Management. 2. Museums—Marketing. 3. Museums—Public
relations. I. Title.

AM121.W35 2010
  069'.068—dc22   2009030796

∞™ The paper used in this publication meets the minimum requirements of American National Standard for Information Sciences—Permanence of Paper for Printed Library Materials, ANSI/NISO Z39.48-1992.

Printed in the United States of America

Contents

Introduction:
Observational Research
versus the Other Researches

It all started at the Hirschhorn Museum and Sculpture Garden in Washington, D.C. It's a round building: the galleries are circular, and when one gets off the escalator at any floor, you can turn right or left. But which? This was intriguing, and when I asked a guard which way most people turned, he didn't know. I myself turned right, counterclockwise, but for six years I wondered what other people did. And I was surprised that a round museum hadn't addressed this dilemma and discussed the implications with all relevant staff. I came to realize that museums have little time for such observations and that I did. Amazingly, an observer of visitors' behavior could uncover all sorts of preferences and rituals, and you didn't have to look long. The other types of research didn't begin to probe what visitors really do, and staffs don't spend precious meeting time on speculation.

In addition to turning right, visitors also hold hands, fidget, chat up the guards, and take funny photos, behaving in many revealing ways that beg for more research to be conducted. Observational research is easy and inexpensive and leads to insights so significant that insight-driven marketing has quickly ascended in popularity among marketers and is unmatched by surveys and focus groups. This emergent method of consumer research has innumerable virtues and simple methods. In the next chapters, you'll be exposed to visitor behaviors, their implications, some discussion guides and optional drill-down research that any museum, of any size or budget, can utilize.

INSIGHT-DRIVEN MARKETING

With observational research, visitor studies professionals can mine more actionable information on how to retain visitors, attract more like them, and convert all of them into repeat purchasers, members, and loyal supporters. The key term is "actionable information" because an essential adjunct to observation is follow-up discussion. *Anyone* in your museum can—and should—take thirty minutes to observe visitors in every location within your domain; *everyone* should gather for sixty minutes to discuss the ramifications. It's the combined observing plus discussion that provides the insights that, for marketers in particular and everyone with a stake in the museum in general, are so golden.

Focus groups, surveys, and one-on-one interviews supply basic information on audiences and help hone and improve a museum's offerings. Observational research provides much deeper, richer knowledge by evaluating not only what visitors say but also what they do in the actual environment of the museum. Observational research studies your ideal consumers—the customers you already have—as they interact inside, spontaneously, with your institution. When you see how visitors behave inside your walls, along your paths, at all your museum's touchpoints, it's easy to understand how they might become more engaged, more satisfied, and more committed to your brand. To watch your visitors, to really observe how they act, is to gain a deeper understanding into their pleasures and needs and how your museum can uniquely fulfill them. Observational research uncovers a treasure trove of subtle human attitudes that abundantly supplement the psychographics gleaned from other forms of research. We've already learned from surveys about lifestyles: travels taken, magazines on the nightstand, who skis, and who goes to theme parks. We've learned about people's motivations outside the museum. Observational research shows us what they do inside with their preferences and predilections. Most significantly, we discover human natures we never imagined.

Observational research refers to studies made in the actual environment of the people being researched. It has usually meant their homes or workplaces, but the terminology also applies to any environment where targeted activities take place, such as a museum. If you want to learn how your visitors act and react, you set up observations in the museum. One of the hallmarks of observational research is that anyone can do it, everyone can discuss the implications of it, and it never requires the high cost of a professional researcher.

SERENDIPITOUS OBSERVATIONS

Observational research is often counterintuitive and therefore provocative. For example, who would have guessed that audiences are happy waiting in lines and that this phenomenon can be turned to good advantage? Looking for answers, you may stumble into more questions. Unlike front-end evaluations, which are useful in projecting outcomes and deservedly popular with exhibition planners and budget minders alike, observational research is directional. You can't use it to estimate the popularity of an exhibition or the effectiveness of a specific exhibit, but you can reliably count on it to load you with insights you can act on. In fact, it may protect you from making bad mistakes based on traditionally good assumptions. As a senior staffer from a West Coast natural history museum said, we tend to ask the questions we already know the answers to. The people being observed don't wait for your questions. The director of a Midwest science museum, a veteran of many focus groups, adds that there's a difference between what moderators ask and what really concerns focus group participants. When you see how people behave, you'll know exactly what concerns them.

British museums already use observational research to deconstruct the anatomy of the museum experience. According to Sylvia Matiko, speaking at the American Association of Museums National Conference in a 2008 panel presentation, "Quantifying Fun," one museum watched children walk tentatively into a barn, pet the animals, giggle with their friends, pose in silly positions, and then relax and talk about the experience in the restaurant. This observational research found that the sequence of behavior eloquently described the learning journey, certainly better than interviewing the child or surveying the parents.

IN SUPPORT OF FRESH IDEAS

The range of observational research is limitless. The more you look, the more you see. And the endlessly original actions of human beings spur creativity in the observers. Observational research supports new thinking from every stakeholder in the museum universe: curators, collections management, exhibition design, operations, education, promotion, finance, complementary programming, trustees, marketing, Web design, funders, sponsors, chief executive officers (CEOs), directors, human resources, and all internal decision makers. Brave new ideas don't have to frighten the bosses. Even at the conceptual stage, before naysayers start throwing up obstacles, the eyes confirm what the mind has only begun to imagine. That's why observational research is such a strong ally when it comes to proposing and justifying new ideas.

New ideas should emanate from every staffer, and they will if the ideators can back them with some research. Curators create highly original exhibitions all the time and then have to justify them to administrators. The education department develops interpretive and cooperative programs and then must defend the extra budget. One of the matchless values of observational research is the supporting evidence it gives to untried ideas and not only from the expected quarters. New ideas are everybody's business; it's this multidiscipline approach that creates a robust museum. Observational research is a staunch defender when staffers defend their ideas to directors and directors then face the questions and skepticism of trustees and funders. Trustees are pushing museums to know more about the market, says Heather Calvin from the Museum of Science in Boston, so as to better match investment with return. Observational research deepens the acquaintanceship with the market.

SURVEYING NON–SURVEY TAKERS
Observational research provides important information that visitor studies cannot. Visitor studies surveys get information from people willing to complete the survey. But what about people who spend most of the visit taking photographs of the stunning architecture? Or people who cross your threshold but never really engage enough to complete a questionnaire? Observational research also offers hints of what's going on in the minds of people who didn't plan the trip, might not plan to return, and might not think of becoming a member. Yet if these people have, however casually, entered your venue, they're prospects and worth knowing better. Observational research forces you to heed the people who walk into a museum store, look around, but don't buy. It compels you to analyze the actions of visitors on guided tours—and this is painful—who look bored. These visitors have come to purchase, either merchandise or learning, and may claim to be satisfied, but if they don't appear joyful, they're unlikely to become loyal. Observational research introduces you to the people who don't pick up the survey form and stubby pencil, the people who respect you enough to pass through but don't love you enough to become a member.

MIND MAPPING AND IDEA GENERATION

As for the emerging interest in mind mapping, new ideas will always define the best museums, and here observational research really has no equal. Ideas, in the history of man, have always come from adaptation and borrowing, from observing what works and what falters. Sparks fly and insights develop when people look around and let the neural networks open up to traffic. Conjecture and that most wonderful of phrases, "what if?," occur when human beings put aside routine tasks and embrace the unexpected. Surveys too often ask the same old questions, resulting in the same old ideas. How often do you need to know where people heard about your museum? How insightful is it to learn that a visitor's satisfaction ranged somewhere between "extremely" and "not very"? Focus groups, as everyone knows, can turn sour if one participant intimidates the others or if everyone falls into groupthink. Even in ideal groups, where the facilitator keeps everyone on task, most of the discussion will evolve along predetermined lines of inquiry, with little time for the "eureka" moment. Observational research will always uncover gold. New ideas emerge painfully, and it is never easy to break from the tried and true, but what will assuage the busy museum professional is how stress free it is to indulge in observational research.

One of the first museum lessons, of course, is that museums are for the many, not only the elite. Everybody knows you can't simply set out the display case and watch the crowds form. What everybody doesn't know is the importance of watching those crowds. Watch the people who crowd the doors fifteen minutes before they open because that's when the public transportation delivered them. Observe the people in the lobby lines who smile. Scan the restaurant and see who is eating with whom. Watch the interactions between visitors. There are many stories that you might not be familiar with but that can be learned through their actions.

CEOS MIGHT NOT LIKE OBSERVATIONS, BUT THEY SHOULD

Observational research will strike an off note with many museum administrators accustomed to designing and/or approving only research that has a stated purpose. As Victor Rabinovitz, CEO of Canadian Museum of Civilization, Gatineau, Quebec, says, visitor studies customarily declare desired outcomes using established metrics. So what to do about observational research, which indulges open-ended looking and speculation? While it's true that observational research requires an open mind on the part of its observers and unfettered creativity from those who gather to mind map and evaluate the implications of it, observational research does have goals, desired outcomes, target audiences, and measurements. The goal: deeper customer knowledge and retention. The desired outcome: actionable insights. The target audience: the customer you already have. The metrics: how many new ideas did we get today? Like all museum research, the measurements aren't always what CEOs hope for, and the implications are not always followed up on immediately. But the data are collectible and actionable.

If you are a conscientious museum marketer, with the budget and the time for front-end, formative, summative, and remedial research, don't dismiss these acknowledged methods. Insight-driven marketing can only sharpen their findings. As consultant Alan Friedman exhorts his clients, put your conclusions out on the floor and see how real visitors use them—to which I add the necessary corollary: put yourself out on the floor.

BRANDING YOUR MUSEUM FOR SUSTAINABILITY AND GROWTH

On the floor is where you'll find members in the making. It's one thing to advertise and promote and attract visitors. It's another thing to convert these customers into repeat purchasers, the loyal supporters who engage with everything you offer. Watch the people who are already inclined to support you—the visitors who stop a few minutes longer at an exhibit, relax at the café, or ask questions of the docent. Observe who smiles a lot, who acts animated, who gushes about a store purchase. These are the people who will return, spread the word, and write a check. In noticing what sparks visitor interest, you'll be identifying new ways to bolster your brand distinctiveness in the leisure marketplace.

Above all, observational research aids retention: learning what *our* visitors really like about their experience with *our* museum so that we can make them ever more loyal to *us*. The desired outcome: sustaining your museum brand. In every chapter of this book, observational research is put in the service of your core values. All observations, all implications, all suggestions lead inexorably to strengthening your mission.

REAL PEOPLE, SENSITIVE ISSUES

Observational research, observing how people really behave inside your museum, throws a spotlight on visitors in the real situation, not in focus group conference room, on the telephone days later, or at their computer in the middle of the night. Observational research reveals information you'd never glean in a visitor survey and would never even ask. You'd never ask a visitor if he uses a cane or is unsteady on her feet. You couldn't ask a five-year-old child what he sees when he walks through a museum holding grandpa's hand. A respondent would have trouble remembering which store item she reached for first or studied longest. Yet answers to these questions open up some different thinking on your market and direct everything from the number of benches you provide to the height of your labels to the style of store furnishings.

Observational research trumps other forms of research when you need to know more than your market's cultural choices and demographics. You might learn from a written questionnaire that current customers also enjoy the symphony and graduated from college; observational research will tell you how they respond to docent tours and how many men actually do come to visit.

Written surveys are starting to ask more behavioral questions, like who accompanies the visitor on museum trips, but only observational research snapshots how these companions actually interact with each other. Who would have guessed that many visitors hold hands as they wander through the exhibits? And here's a new opportunity: all those people—friends and relatives—who accompany the respondent. "Listening" to the opinions of not only the decision maker of the day's expedition but also the others accesses a very important target: hard-to-get prospects that are now actually inside the door. Supplied with these insights, a museum can assess and plan everything from the height of labels to floor layout to mailing ZIP codes.

SMALL MUSEUM OR LARGE, ANY SIZE CAN PLAY

Observational research gives any museum, of any size, genre, or structure, a wider view of operations because you have to get out of your office and move around. Small museums, whose staffs wear many hats, benefit mightily from sharing the visitor studies responsibility. You can assign any staffer to take off thirty minutes, whenever that time is available, to simply observe. When the staff is only two or three people, for whom blue-sky meetings are a luxury, watching visitors substitutes nicely. And since the goal here is insights, not specific solutions, you can even conduct observations in another, larger museum. The best news of all for small museums is that observational research is free and doesn't require a bevy of experts to analyze it.

For larger museums, observations open the doors between departments. Multidepartment museums have discovered that the squares and circles on the organization chart can no longer be siloed, that curatorial and development and collections and visitor services must, instead, correlate their activities for maximum impact and economy. The departments must talk to each other to understand their shared purpose. Many visitor behaviors observed in one area of the museum have relevance for another, and the thinking of many helps fine-tune the tasks of those most responsible. For example, the same phenomenon of hand-holding pertains not only in the galleries but in the store as well. Thirty-inch-tall children have implications for wall labels as well as marketing brochures. The numerical strength of the Frail and Hardy will echo in the development department, volunteer office, and marketing lists.

Most museums already act interdepartmentally. The museum store, for example, selects its merchandise to reflect the current exhibition and ideally starts the buying process at about the same time that the curators start to plan a show. The education department develops special programs to augment membership. Volunteers answer—or at least pass along to the right curator or membership director—questions ranging from the price of a membership to the furniture style in a restored parlor. Holistic thinking really flourishes when you observe the visitor in all of his or her behaviors.

Corporate marketers, not so long ago, added observational research to their box of research tools not only to satisfy customers but also to engage them in making the product better. Watching how women move around the kitchen helps kitchen companies design user-friendlier appliances and easier-to-study package instructions. Watching TV viewers handle the remote control led to the concept of Wii. Observing which backseat passengers buckled their seat belts dictated automobile design. At Ace Hardware, a front-of-the-store employee is trained to observe body language. He determines which customers like to browse alone, which want help fast, and which have a major project on their minds. He then messages those findings to sales assistants in the aisles so that the appropriate customers are left alone and the others met with a knowledgeable staffer. All these case studies have relevance for museums, and all began with observation.

LISTENING TO YOUR AUDIENCE

As museums evolve the concept of storytelling, observational research will play a role. Think of the original storytellers, who were not only entertaining but respected and loved as well. They endured because, in addition to informing and teaching, they listened and responded. It's the difference between their being satisfactory and their being loved. So when staffers observe how visitors take in their many stories—the design of an exhibition, a guided tour, or the layout of the café—they more correctly understand how to sustain their brand beyond satisfaction, all the way to love and trust. A current master storyteller, actor and author Steve Martin, conducted his own version of observational research. In his book *Born Standing Up*, he tells how he studied audiences in comedy clubs for the way they reacted to his bits. He created a new type of audience-centric comedy that scholars have praised for the past thirty years. He went on to act and write with much-lauded sensitivity; yes, he knew how to deliver a line and turn a phrase, but he knew more than most what audiences wanted. The fact that Martin is also an accomplished art collector adds frosting to the cake of diligent observing.

Insight-driven marketing helps retain the loyalty of visitors and other constituents and forcefully promotes the hard-earned distinctiveness of your institution. Observational research, engaged in regularly, will provide those insights. The examples in this book are exemplary, but only that. The methodology underpinning them gives you the tools to find your own, and they are limitless. Enjoy the view.

1

Methodology

The observational research described in this book differs in complexity from the traditional discipline, which can involve many stages and steps. Traditional ethnographic research, which began as a study of societies, is a thorough system of observations over a long period of time that are carefully documented, hypothesized, sometimes quantified and always analyzed, but not usually subjected to "what-ifs." Museum market researchers can't afford the time and cost of this intensive research and will want to advance quickly to the discussion of what-ifs and experimenting with new ideas. The goal of observational research for museum marketers is not mere study but also ideas and action.

The first step in observational research is a stated purpose. All good research for marketing starts by asking, "Why are we doing this?" For museums, the purpose is to gain insights into the visitor/consumer that will help the institution retain its loyal constituency and grow. There might be a more proximate reason, such a grant proposal, budget allocation, acquisition, exhibition design, fund-raising campaign, or training program, but ultimately the goal is brand sustainability.

Next, you need an agreement on terms. It must be accepted that this research is not quantifiable, nor does it substitute for information usually gleaned from written or verbal responses. Everyone involved in the project— and that should include administrators as well as the staffers who conduct the research and analyze it—must accept its methodology and limitations.

START BY SIMPLY LOOKING

The research described in this book starts with sitting or standing in a public area of the museum to unobtrusively observe what happens. That includes watching anybody who enters the front door, following (eyes only) individuals as they proceed through the lobby, galleries, and other spaces. It also includes watching a given space, such as the information desk or a store shelf, to see how visitors act in its vicinity. Notes can be taken, if necessary, although discretion recommends storing all observations mentally and writing them down later. At no time should a person "under observation" be approached verbally; at that point, the research would be not observational but rather a one-on-one interview, useful for clarification or designing future research but disastrous for authentic behavior study. In addition, any obtrusiveness requires that you ask the individual's permission first.

BELIEVE WHAT YOU SEE

Observation should be totally open minded. The goal is to see what there is to be seen. Observers can and should conduct corroborative observations in different circumstances at different times to bolster first impressions and also to disprove them, but you must be prepared to believe in what you see.

The time allotted for observing depends on the size of the observation area and the patience of the observer. Exciting findings have been realized after watching a gallery for five minutes. Usually it takes less than thirty minutes to find patterns of behavior that surprise. Most watchers can verify their initial reactions in forty-five minutes. That is, in the first few minutes you'll see a behavior that surprises you, such as visitors reaching the end of a long line and actually smiling and thanking the ticket taker. The watcher will continue watching to see if this behavior is repeated. It usually takes no more than half an hour to convince the observer that, indeed, most people hold no grudges for long lines. In no instance should an observation last longer than an hour. Any observation striking enough to cause a ripple in the observer's mind will have occurred by then, and, besides, the observer will be tired. One of the hallmarks of observational research for museum marketers is that the studies can be usefully accomplished in no more than an hour at a time.

VARIABLES

For actionable marketing intelligence, methodological integrity demands that observers double-check their observations, preferably under different variables, such as time of day, day of week, seasonality, and current exhibition(s). Professional marketers talk about "drill-down," probing deeper into any issue not immediately clear. A museum may want to quantify the information, especially if it's to be used for grant proposals or budget requests. Surprising or counterintuitive findings may need the clarification that focus groups provide. Sometimes an observation will quickly blossom into multiple observations, raising the quantity of questions that only large-scale surveys or intensive individual interviews can answer. Observational research was never intended to stand alone.

THINKING WEIRD

The most important phase of the methodology is the postresearch discussion, analysis, and evaluation. Whether there are resources for costly multidimensional research or just thirty minutes of staff time at the Monday morning meeting, the value of observational research comes from the discussions it generates and the implications it suggests. The analysis/discussion phase includes brainstorming and hypothesizing about the findings, drawing first-draft conclusions, and projecting rational outcomes.

Wondering "what if" and speculating on "what could be" is not for everyone. Accountants tend to be poor daydreamers. Conversely, exhibition designers overflow with creative blue-skying. Many staffers think best inside the box, and many others, though inclined to leap outside the box, have been warned to justify before they jump. Observational research requires that everybody put on jumping shoes and leap into unknown territory. Weird ideas must become the province of everybody, not only the "creative types," because in the museum, many of the new thinking will affect quotidian topics like seating in the lobby or employees in the cafeteria. All new product successes, especially the ones beloved by comptrollers and shareholders, seemed bizarre at one point. Selling coffee in bookstores is one that comes quickly to mind, and this strange idea became mainstream very quickly. Thinking weird is not difficult, but forcing unusual ideas from the brain to the lips and saying it to a group of peers takes skills that not everyone has. Some museums hire facilitators for a few hours to do just that: to inspire and motivate and coax out the gold that lurks inside all human minds. The reason for the cliché of "no bad ideas" is that everyone has original ideas all the time, and there's no way to predict which will turn out the best.

The twentieth-century suggestion box was a managerial philosophy that still works. The twenty-first-century buzzword "scenario" also should be brought out into the open more often. Asking colleagues to imagine different scenarios encourages more than fresh ideas: it sends the message that there are always multiple ways to run a museum and demonstrates the validity in all of them.

DOCUMENTATION

The final or next-to-final stage in the observational research process is a written document. For many museums, the insights gained will be fascinating, even transformational, but not immediately executable. However, they must be documented and circulated. Even the shortest period of observation, even one-off observations, can lead to new ideas. This exercise in open-minded thinking alone justifies the effort. Documenting your observations comes in handy later if you want to dig deeper into the people and situations you've observed. It's called drilling down, and it gained credence when researchers discovered how much information lay beneath the streams of data collected digitally. Actually, you have drilled beneath the surface already, thanks to your observations and group discussions. But if you have questions that need clarifying or just a lot of curiosity, you can follow up with focus groups, questionnaires, surveys, one-on-one interviews, or online probes. And you can do all these things relatively inexpensively.

DRILL-DOWN METHODS

Lucky for museums, you have focus group participants coming through your door every day and databases of people who have already demonstrated their interest. Since all the drill-down methods require museum-focused participants, recruit on the spot. You can leave sign-up cards at the information desk, museum store, café or restaurant, kiosks, rest stations, or exhibition areas, where appropriate. You can place electronic sign-up cards on laptops at secure places throughout the museum. Ask docents or guides, again where appropriate and not contrary to education procedures, to solicit participants.

Publicize in your newsletters that special interest groups will be assembled to discuss ongoing activities at the museum; this, like all research, has the added value of awareness and newsworthiness.

FOCUS GROUPS

Focus groups are popular because they tackle one issue at a time and get like-minded people together to stimulate and compare ideas. They don't provide answers or give quantitative data, but they do corroborate intuitions and propose valid new directions. The moderator can be from within or outside the museum but should speak of the museum in the third person and state his or her neutrality at the outset. If you record or film the session, you must notify the respondents at the beginning, and if they are uncomfortable, pay them anyway (if you have agreed to the standard fee in your area) and send them home. If any respondent gets feisty or dominates the group unduly, you may want to dismiss him or her with pay. The agenda of a focus group breaks down into four areas: 1) introduce your topic and ask everyone for his or her first name plus any information they want to provide; every newly assembled group, whether it's a European walking tour or a professional workshop, does this; 2) discuss museums in general just to make sure that everyone is on the same page; 3) ask specific questions about the topic of focus; and 4) probe the answers of individual responses. The introductions and general comments warm the group up. The next questions get to the heart of the inquiry.

Be prepared to pay anything from $10 to $100 or an in-kind gift such as a book or packet of passes. If you're recruiting women who work outside the home and have stricter schedules, you'll pay on the higher side. Professional people or narrow categories like maritime historians will cost more because the pool is smaller. It's very hard to recruit chefs and actors because they work nontraditional hours. The most productive sessions last one and a half to two hours—long enough to elicit a range of ideas and probe them but not so long as to disintegrate into tedium.

Focus group moderators introduce themselves as neutral parties and stay that way. Ideally, they are outside professionals, not museum staffers. Most moderators begin the session by saying, "I am here to listen to your thoughts, whatever they are. My feelings will not be hurt by anything you say, so please speak frankly. All your comments will be kept confidential. I do not work for the client; I have been hired by the client to hear what you have to say."

However, it's acceptable to use your own personnel if they present themselves as totally objective.

Provide water (at the very least), soft drinks, and coffee. Snacks are optional, depending on the time of day. If you do provide food, have everyone eat before the discussion starts so that they can talk easily. Focus groups cost money, and you don't want to waste time. Professionally moderated groups are recorded so that the moderator can listen carefully without having to take notes. Customarily, no one else is in the room, and many facilities have one-way-glass facilities so that others can view and listen to the proceedings. If you conduct sessions in-house and want one or two administrators to sit in, keep them far in the background and do not allow them to talk or ask questions. After fifteen minutes, the moderator can step outside and check to make sure the conversation is headed the right direction. After an hour or so, he or she can step outside again to see if there are further issues to explore.

When the session is finished, thank the participants sincerely and ask if they have any questions. This is polite and politic; they must not feel exploited, and they have a right to fully understand how their comments will be used. Assure them again that this information stays within the museum. Realize that they are either current or prospective visitors and explain how important they are to the museum's service to the public. Don't forget to obtain their written consent or to hand out their fee.

ONE-ON-ONE INTERVIEWS

A variant of the focus group is the one-on-one interview. This can be conducted like a mall intercept by stopping a likely target and asking if you can take fifteen to thirty minutes of his or her time to ask a few questions. The rule here is ironclad: be polite, apologize for intruding, back off immediately if there is any hint of resistance, disclose the reasons for the interview and exactly how their responses will be used, state the length of the interview and stick to it, and get written consent.

SURVEYS

You can distribute written surveys at various points in the museum, depending on your size, interior design, and staff. If you provide a stack of questionnaires at the information desk, decide whether to have staff hand them out personally, put up a "please take one" sign, or just leave them out. You could distribute them at the museum store checkout, at the restaurant checkout, or at tables throughout the museum. If you have large grounds and rest stations, that might be a good opportunity for visitors to rest and reflect on your questions. For museums with internal transportation, trams, or shuttle buses and the rides are long enough, that might be a good place to distribute short questionnaires or to announce them. Printed programs, available at lectures or performances, are an excellent way to distribute questionnaires, especially if there's an intermission or early entry; people love to have something to do while waiting. There may even be occasions when your docents or guides can distribute questionnaires, even though you will have little background information on the respondents.

ONLINE SURVEYS

Online surveys have the advantage of convenience—for you and the respondent—and spontaneity: they can be completed whenever the online viewer wants. These surveys allow for more questions and open-ended responses; it's much easier to type answers than to write them. In addition, if you aren't getting useful information, it's easy to go back into the site and rephrase the questions. The main disadvantage is scope: you reach many more unqualified respondents than qualified ones, and it wastes time to sort the wheat from the chaff. Online respondents skew differently than the ones contacted in the museum: conventional wisdom says that they are younger, work best late at night, have nothing better to do, are venturesome and forward looking, and are too tech-savvy. They are, by definition, a little harder to identify. They are not, however, extraordinary. The profile of the online user has changed greatly in the past few years and continues to change daily. The main danger with online surveys is the temptation to dumb them down and continue to ask the same superficial questions asked in conventional surveys. Embrace the new technology and use it creatively to unlock motivations and behaviors that may not be disclosed in person.

Each method of distribution constitutes a variable that might affect the type of respondent or quality of response, but any will yield additional insights. Just be sure to keep a record of how the questionnaires were distributed and when, including date and time. Record how you assemble any focus group, one-on-one interview, or online survey so that you can explain the results. Research can be very upsetting in that it overturns convenient truths, and it helps to assess the findings in view of the many variables. These variables enrich every piece of information you gather.

You'll find suggested "drill-down" research methods at the end of every chapter. They include specific guidelines and questions for a wide range of research techniques: intercept questionnaires, passive surveys, electronic surveys, sales receipts, competitions, empathy sessions, facilitated employee discussions, one-on-one interviews, brainstorming, and a wide variety of focus groups. Whether you choose to drill deeper into visitor insights, these guidelines will shed light on what you've already observed. Also, the suggested research can be conducted as stand-alone inquiries. Each drill-down method can be adapted to the size, scope, and immediate goals of your institution, and can be implemented by existing staff at little additional cost.

2

The Hand-Holders: Connecting to Your Museum

It was a balmy summer evening at the Chicago Botanic Garden, Glencoe, Illinois, where salsa music played on the Esplanade and fragrance floated on every breeze. Along the paths, countless couples were holding hands. Of course, an idyllic setting will engender tender touches, but these observations were remarkable in their quantity. Subsequent observations revealed that visitors hold hands not only during Watteauesque evenings but also during the day, throughout the following cold months, and even when walking from the parking lot. People hold hands in winter with mittens on. Even in the museum store, there they are, holding hands. And this touching scenario plays out in all kinds of museums, in all seasons, around the world.

Observation from the vantage points of lobbies, entranceways, and outdoor benches reveals a new Age of Aquarius, with museumgoers engaged in all types of intimate behavior: holding hands, leaning into each other, bumping shoulders, and talking raptly face-to-face. The couples holding hands are young and old, parents and children. The attached couples include moms with teenagers, friends with friends. What is striking is that almost everyone who visits a museum with a companion talks intimately with that friend; the interaction is close and joyous. People talk and touch as they enter the museum, they gesture and discuss on leaving, and they stick close together most of the time in between. Hand-holding can be observed frequently at art museums, botanic gardens, and historic houses but tapers off at heritage and science museums. It seems to flourish where exhibits are visual. Where labels and panels contribute to the communication of an exhibit, where visitors might read at different speeds or different degrees, the hands let go of each other. But the phenomenon holds across cultures, in museums from the United States to Italy, China, and Australia.

What is it about a museum that encourages such companionable togetherness? An obvious answer is sociability, one of the main reasons people visit museums. Many college students say that they go to museums on dates; it's something to do, and it's cheap. But that's not the whole story because older married couples and well-dressed cool couples and senior couples also hold hands, lean into each other, and touch to draw the other's attention to an exhibit. No, something in the atmosphere and content of a museum must resonate deeply to appeal so strongly to the heart.

When observational research discovers a phenomenon like hand-holding, it begs further attention, primarily because it's so widespread and unique. Few visitors hold hands at the theater perhaps because, as an actress and college professor points out, the theater presents issues and conflicts, and audiences come to the venue prepared to be confronted. At symphonic musical performances, there's some hand-holding, but the proximity is forced by the fact of seats, and obviously the lights are off. At opera performances, where drama illustrates the music, there is less hand-holding. Even in the lobbies, where everyone effulges in animated conversation, the groupings are foursomes, not couples, and there is very little twosome intimacy. The brazen togetherness exhibited in wide-open museum spaces is *sui generis* and of too great a magnitude to ignore. And because this behavior seems to occur mainly in museums as opposed to other arts venues, it's a competitive advantage to be studied and nurtured.

IMPLICATIONS OF CLOSENESS

The implications of physical closeness and heartfelt, engaged conversation reach into every corner of a museum's domain, giving brainstorming sessions plenty of raw data to mine further. Think about how comfortable closeness affects the placement of exhibits and labels or the pacing of tours. Educators, who know that students of any age learn well from their peers, might rethink the structure of tours so that couples could talk to each other in the galleries without having to sidestep the tour. Such a wise museum might redesign wall labels so that each member of the couple could read at the same time.

Consider the affect of shoulder-to-shoulder couples in the museum store; you might want to widen the aisles. In the restaurant, you might replace the four-tops with tables for two and extend hours of operation to accommodate serious conversations; when museums beguile people into rapt conversations, their restaurants and cafés become an important place for friends to pause and share experiences. When the Toledo Art Museum placed notices on its refreshment nook tables to "relax, reflect, discuss," it must have known that companionable visitors are wont to do just that. The marketing department might try to collect names of companions so that materials are sent to both visitors to the museum, not just the friend who took the initiative. Note that many of the friendly couples are just that, friends or parents with older children, and that while the visit ends up being a togetherness event, it frequently starts as a one-person initiative.

In developing new market segments, coupleness suggests many more categories of visitors than conventionally recognized on traditional surveys. No segmentation study can adequately comprehend the psychographics of companionship. Observation suggests that museums actually attract many distinct segments of visitors, such as mothers with college-age children, forty-something women who lunch with the girls, and that much-desired segment of disposable-income individuals called old married couples. When you look beyond the obvious, you'll view grade school teachers not merely as chaperones of school tours but as young people who go on dates.

POWER OF TWO

The power of two reemerges in the museum store, where the love of shopping intensifies when there's another person to share it with. Women, particularly, love to share the thrill of the purchase, but evidence shows that many kinds of couples shop in tandem in the museum store, and there are more male shoppers than you'll ever see on most shopping trips. It may take further research to prove that two people spend twice as much as one, but prudence suggests getting both names for the database and stocking more male merchandise. Even if men don't shop, the conventional wisdom of the department store couch—the place where men can slump so that women can shop unimpeded—also applies at museum stores. One museum calls them the "man chairs." A couple-sensitive museum would certainly explore two-for-one entries, offers for out-of-town relatives, and a deeper database. Certainly there's a chance that two will shop more passionately than one.

Taking a closer look at twosomes highlights a critical advantage of observational research over focus groups or surveys. Most traditional research participants are singletons, and they are strongly encouraged to answer questions, whether on a survey or in a focus group, by themselves. Often, the person answering the questions is the dominant half of the twosome, the one who suggested the visit and made the plans. So, marketers never hear the impressions of the person who tags along, who may be a casual visitor or first-timer but is deeply engaged in hand-in-hand viewing. Now that you've watched couples and twosomes and appreciated the depth of togetherness, you can design further research to better understand this segment.

DRILL-DOWN
A simple and inexpensive questionnaire, distributed to anyone visiting as part of a twosome, will yield immediate information you've probably never had before. Ask the following:

Who are you visiting with today (e.g., friend, relative, out-of-town guest)?

What aspects of the museum did you agree on (likes or dislikes)?

Were there any parts of the museum where you differed in opinions?

Thinking of people with whom you enjoy spending time, who might be interested in accompanying you to this museum in the future?

What would you and your friend like to change about this visit?

What other leisure activities do you two enjoy together?

We're giving you a $6 store discount certificate as thanks for taking this time to speak to us. Will you share it or split it $3 each?

There are four advantages to this kind of questionnaire:

Feedback on how your museum can better serve twosomes

Additional time after the visit when the twosome together can discuss and reflect on their experience

Names of both parties and their addresses, if different.

Damage control (It's bad enough when one person has a complaint; when there are two people, the problem is magnified and recalled for a much longer time. The comment card airs the issue immediately and disarms it.)

FOCUS ON COUPLES

Couples-oriented focus groups are rare because it's hard to coordinate a couple's schedule; they're also expensive. However, their unusualness guarantees that the participants will offer fresh insights. Alternatively, you could convene a group of solo participants and filter for those who visit museums in a pair. After the usual preliminaries of introductions, probe for the motivations of visiting museums as a couple by asking the following:

Do you always visit museums as a couple?

What makes this so pleasant?

What are the disadvantages, if any?

Do you collaborate on what to see, when to go, and how long to stay? Or does one person plan the visit?

Whom do you visit a museum with? (Name everyone: spouse, date, friend, relative, colleague)

Why do you think it's more fun as a twosome?

Are some museums more enjoyable to visit alone?

What's the main reason you visit a museum?

Do you learn more or get more enjoyment when you visit with someone else?

What other leisure activities do you enjoy together? (Prompt: theater, movies, restaurants, library, symphony, opera, concerts, lectures)

Will you use the free tickets/discount coupons together?

An important benefit of couples focus groups is the opportunity to observe how they interact with each other. Listen to their comments and also watch their body language. As with any focus group, include free tickets or discount coupons with the participant payment.

Remember that focus groups are directional, not summative. You won't get solutions to problems. You won't get definitive answers to questions. The insights cannot be projected to a large group because the research sample in an eight- or ten-person session is so small. And just when you think you're homing in on a chosen topic, the group will blurt out something totally new and provocative, and you'll want to follow that lead.

Even if you can't afford the time or money for additional research, this is one area where internal discussions will reap rewards. You need to probe the power of two because two people are better than one, whether they're visitors, members, or donors, and because they frequently support you as a couple. People who spread the word about your institution by starting with "we" are extremely persuasive. You need to explore the power inherent in a museum visit that it can bring people so close together.

3

Twitching on the Tour

People taking tours just might be the least animated people in the museum. You'd think they were lining up to get measured for the military. While waiting for the tour to start, they stand ramrod straight, about three feet from any other person, and look straight ahead. They don't chat and, in fact, studiously avoid anyone else. Are they intellectuals, preparing their minds for the gallery talk and walk to follow? Are they loners, taking group tours because they have no one to go with? They're not bored with the museum, or they wouldn't be waiting to see more of it, and they're probably not boring people. Following these stick figures through the course of the guided tour, another behavioral trait emerges: lack of movement. It's as if the energy has been drained from these men and women: they don't slouch, fidget, or twitch. They don't move from one foot to another, jut out a hip, or sway. They don't whisper to each other or giggle. Unlike almost everybody else in the museum, people who aren't taking a tour and who are twisting and gesturing, the tourers behave like inductees with their first drill sergeant.

In observing many of these loose clusters waiting for a tour to begin and then following the individuals as they move with the guide or docent through the galleries, it is obvious that they aren't loners or losers, intense intellectuals, or opinionless robots. The have companions and ask good questions, but what emerges is a person slightly drained of spirit.

Attitudes toward tours have been studied before, and one can logically weigh the pros and cons of guided tours versus independent visiting. Now it's time to look more closely at the people who actually do take tours. Whatever they may say later about the value of their tour experience, how they act reveals how they feel, and in today's marketing world, how customers feel is becoming very important. Surveys may reveal that the tour is informative, the guide knowledgeable, and the sixty minutes devoted to it well worth the time. This may indicate a satisfied visitor. However, it is much more important to have a happy visitor, one who is energized by the museum, its exhibits, and its people. A museum should strive for oxygenated visitors, people so enlivened that they can't wait tell their friends, come back often, buy a book, or, perhaps, support this institution that has so inspired them. You want a visitor who has tasted champagne, not one who has finished his or her milk.

BREATH OF FRESH AIR

On visits to two contemporary art museums, on different ends of the country, the mood of the touring visitors was decidedly phlegmatic. Most were close-mouthed, unresponsive except when taking part in discussions, and almost glum looking. They stood and moved stiffly. Of the sometimes fifteen people who now and then gathered around the lecturer, a few occasionally broke into smiles and animation, but the general attitude was of statuary. Everyone stood motionless—arms akimbo, hands clasped formally, or hands stuffed in pockets; feet planted firmly and straight forward, weight evenly distributed, and spine straight. When other visitors joined the tour on a room-by-room basis, fresh air breezed in with them.

Contrast this with people walking through the galleries on their own: one foot forward, hip jutted, posture shifting; motioning, touching, gesturing; people looking at work and chatting with companions, talking with their hands; bodies swiveled toward each other and back to the exhibit; swaying and rocking back on their heels, sometimes twisting to look at something else or putting their heads together to discuss what was in front of them, always at one angle or another. You don't have to be a coach or dance therapist to believe that working one's muscles helps the mind to work, too.

SOME TOUR GROUPS SURPRISE YOU

It's no secret that some exhibitions attract more tourers than others, and in such popular shows, the tours might, in fact, work against that vibe. A recent rock-and-roll blockbuster hauled in waves of the nostalgic, and the tide of visitors raised the number of tours as well. But though the guides were well versed in the intricacies of 1960s music and culture, it turned out that most group members found more joy in reminiscing with each other. It was a common bond that had visitors talking for weeks after, and that's about the best thing that can happen to a museum. The tour was appreciated, but the behavior said, "Let us just have our reunion with each other." There are times to step back and let the engagement happen without you.

In fact, sometimes a show with cultural energy benefits from the strength of the group. A retrospective of African American artist Kerry James Marshall attracted huge crowds, and many black social organizations came as groups, some museum tours reaching thirty people. Here the group dynamic sparkled. Conversation played back and forth between members of the group, and interaction grew between individuals and the guide. Far from stolid, these tour groups vibrated. So there are many kinds of groups: some listen intently and motionlessly, some talk and interact, and some disperse. After observing all the variations in touring groups, one lesson is clear: be adaptable. If you assess behaviors on a group-by-group basis and realize that no one style of touring fits all groups, you can nurture the right kind of energy in all.

ACTIONS

Of course, there are logical explanations for why some visitors in group tours seem so severe. One must not talk during a lecture by the tour guide, except to ask a question or answer one. And if one has decided to devote a whole hour to a tour, one will stand up straight and listen. Listening to words that describe something visual requires a different kind of attentiveness than does looking at the visual itself. Docents can offset this seriousness by taking a pause and letting visitors just look at the exhibit; if it's a three-dimensional work, encourage them to walk around it. At some point in the tour, the guide can tell everyone to look around the room and even spread out and then say, "I'll meet you in the next gallery." Even if some wander off, the group dynamic will be more alert.

Another reason for staying so upright and uptight: sometimes, a person just feels shy about acting out in front of this ensemble that, for a brief period, is a new social group. In this case, the docent or guide can warm up the group informally a few minutes before start time. Ask where everyone comes from, if they've visited the museum before, and what similar museums or exhibitions they've seen. If you're lucky, there will be a "connector" in the tour, a person who is not reticent, who asks a few (but not too many) questions, who nods at the docent's comments, and who connects with the docent. The guide can liven up the whole group by directing a few comments at this person: "Let's ask the gentleman from Pittsburgh how he would use this canoe." Remember that visiting a museum is an individual experience, and the more guides address the individuals, the less those individuals will fall into group lassitude.

Other variables that might explain or excuse group rigidity could be the exhibition itself, the time of day, the season of the year, or the weather outside. If further research indicates one of these obstacles, docents can adjust their opening remarks accordingly. A docent might lead off with, "This is a scholarly look at the artist's body of work so stop me if I get too professorish," or "On such a cold, wet day, you'll find it bright and cheerful in here," or "Are you here on spring break? How's it going this semester?" Again, just because it's a group tour doesn't mean you can't talk to the congregate as individuals.

A brief understanding of proxemics—the study of how people position themselves in relation to others—will help you evaluate touring. Some people and cultures like proximity. Some tolerate it, and some can't stand it. As museums reach out to ever more diverse visitors and as more cultures, local and foreign, reach out to you, realize that closeness to others is one of only many needs you'll confront.

Here's a counterintuitive observation: animated guides may beget static listeners. A docent who is full of background information, interesting anecdotes, and details may, by force of personality, compensate for the lack of spirit in the group and unknowingly facilitate the continuing dyspepsia.

IMPLICATIONS OF MOTIONLESSNESS

At this point, you may well wonder what's so terrible about a motionless tour. After all, they stay until the end, spend at least forty-five minutes inside the museum, receive value added, and are probably the type to follow up with a purchase in the bookstore, not to mention go home with favorable comments to friends. Like any behavior, lack of motion is a danger signal if the majority of visitors exhibit an excess of it.

The first purpose of a guided tour is education, and you can question how, if the body is stiff and rigid, the mind can process the excitement of knowledge. In the totality of the museum experience, learning plays a huge role, and visiting learners need more than simply hearing a lecture; they need to internalize it, understand its relevance, and remember it. Indisputably, some people learn best by hearing, but there may be additional ways to enhance their appreciation.

Another purpose of a guided tour is more cosmetic: it makes the total package look better. A good museum offers tours to prove its promise of interpretation and education, to validate its mission. For all your stakeholders—other visitors, donors, board members, grantors, educators, community, government, and media—tours are a badge of excellence. They need to be continually revitalized and, frankly, to look vital.

From a marketing perspective, every activity of the museum must build support and retain loyalty. Guided tours serve these goals admirably because, conducted in the right way, they embrace casual visitors and convert them in less than an hour into engaged friends. They explain, through personal contact and informal anecdotes, the distinctive personality and significance of your institution.

As a competitor in the world of leisure activities, your museum gives consumers many wonderful reasons to choose you: learning, enrichment, socialization, and entertainment. A tour can be all those things. But as you compete, you need to know more about your product, the tour, and the consumers themselves.

DRILL-DOWN: CUSTOMERS

To gather more information about the success of your touring program, start with the customer, people who have already purchased—in actual money or their valuable time—a visit. So the first piece of research starts with them. Give them comment cards and pencils and ask if they'd be willing to answer two questions about the tour. For this research, you might want to shorten the tour. Ask only one or two questions. Some suggestions are the following:

What will you remember twenty-four hours from now?

If we cut five minutes from this tour, what should we omit?

If we added five minutes, should we add:

Another object (or room in the house, or interactive exhibit—be specific to your museum)

More group discussion

Q & A

Supplemental reading material

Which work/feature/artifact gave you new information or learning?

Other comments:

State at the outset that you're asking for visitors' opinions of the tour, not what they think of the docent. Provide the docent with a small box or large envelope to collect the cards so that the respondents don't worry about confidentiality. To keep the research time short, give half the questions to some groups and half to others.

As an alternative to comment cards, have the docent ask these questions verbally at the end of the tour and request that the docent e-mail them to the education director as soon as possible. E-mail is recommended, as it's immediate and easy and will encourage the docent to answer fully while the words and context are fresh.

Another option is to provide a laptop computer at the information desk, where tour participants can answer a lengthier questionnaire. Although there is a chance that the research will be compromised by respondents other than tourers, you'll still get valuable input.

DRILL-DOWN: CONSUMERS

The difference between a customer and consumer: consumers are customers that you don't have yet. Visitors who don't yet take tours are still prospects, and if they never intend to buy into the idea of a tour, find out why.

Lone rangers, those independents who walk and talk on their own or with one other person, who wander and gesture and frequently strike thinking poses, may be the most fulfilled customers, and they are the very ones who the museum should talk to at some point. They might not take tours but could well be the type to return again and again, sign up for membership, tell their friends, and buy souvenirs to remember the experience. Since tours can be so enriching for this kind of visitor, find out what's unappealing in them. Search out these independent visitors: when you see people leaning toward each other, talking with their hands, and twitching, see if you can't touch them as well. You could identify them in the galleries and hand them a short questionnaire to be filled out any time before they leave. As with group visitors, keep the questions to two per card. Examples are the following:

What exhibits/works/artifacts would you return to look at more closely?

What will you remember twenty-four hours from now?

Suppose you were asked to conduct a fifteen-minute tour for friends. What would you show?

These questions are quite different from the set proposed for group tourers. They will give you a sense of how non–group people navigate your galleries. It would be interesting to give them to groups and see how they differ. As with all research, be prepared to revise the questions as you collect more information. Part of this revision process demands scheduling the research at different times of day, days of the week, and seasons of the year.

LEARNING STYLES
Tours are taken and given as learning experiences, and differences in learning style will account for much of the behavior we see. Docents and guides, who must adapt to both the bored and the restless, will handle their jobs with an easier mind if they understand these learning styles. A recent study sheds much-needed light on four learning styles: visual, aural, read, and kinetic. A student in a classroom learns by looking, hearing, reading, or hands-on doing, and the same matrix applies to learners of any age in museums. It's hard to assess the learning styles of strangers, but some behaviors give an indication of how best to guide them. The wanderer is probably visual, soaking up everything as far as the eye can see. The note taker's behavior probably indicates

a reader. Your traditional tour taker learns well by hearing. And those who move their bodies, pointing and framing, nudging and poking, and twitching their bodies as a nervous substitute for touching, give new meaning to the kinetic learner. Perhaps the next round of research is observing your groups with attention to how they learn. Start with asking what your docents have observed.

DRILL-DOWN: DOCENTS

Brainstorming is inexpensive, pleasant research, and gathering together your docents to compare notes has the added benefit of giving them a voice. It's hard to carve out time for idea generating, and docents and tour guides have a specific job for which they have been carefully trained at no small expenditure of time by hardworking education department professionals. However, their face-to-face interaction with your customers bespeaks another de facto job description: observational feedback.

A similar research format is the focus group. In this case, you'll not only lead a discussion but also drill down and really probe. Like all focus groups, it will focus on one subject: how individuals benefit (or not) from a tour. As with all focus groups, you recruit for participants who share a common interest, in this case guiding tours for all kinds of learners. Don't be tempted to augment the group with other staffers. Although consumer focus groups can be expensive to identify and bring in, this is no problem with your docents. As with all focus groups, this one should follow the structure of introduction, general questions, specific questions, and probing questions based on individual responses. The introductions and general comments warm the group up. The next questions get to the heart of the inquiry.

Some questions you might include in your outline of the docent focus group are the following:

Please tell the group your name and what days/time/type of tour you lead.

What's the most rewarding part of the tour for you?

What do you think is the most rewarding aspect for the visitor?

Thinking back, describe a particularly interesting visitor.

Go back as far as you want and describe a tour that you particularly enjoyed leading.

What exhibits/artifacts/exhibitions have proven best for touring?

Tell us as bad tour experience.

If a friend were interested in becoming a tour docent, what would you tell him or her?

Considering that museum visitors have many choices of leisure and cultural activities, why do you think they choose your museum and your tours?

Keep the questions focused on the tours, not the individual docents. And follow up these open-ended questions with plenty of drill-down. Ask the participants why they said what they said. Ask them to explain further. Ask who else has had a similar experience. Ask why again. To keep the responses flowing frankly, select an outside facilitator or a museum staffer from outside the education department

The "who else?" questions encourage response-to-respondents comments. Here is where focus groups improve on questionnaires, as they prompt a free flow of information, each building on others. Often these responses will provide new questions for you to ask at subsequent focus groups.

Wherever your research leads, be grateful to restless tourers who come and go; they are embracing and absorbing your museum. Be aware that nontwitchers may need extra stimulation to convert them from being coolly satisfied to being warmly engaged. It can be disconcerting for a tour guide when people appear to lose interest, but in this case, appearances are misleading. Museum visitors wander off from acuity, not boredom; they are interested, attentive people who are checking out the total museum, not just a given course.

Look around and thrill at the wondrous ways of your visitors. Remember that observational research provides invaluable insights and that whatever you see is good.

4

Sitting Down

It was the secondary entrance of the museum, a large lobby where the auditorium, restrooms, and education department classrooms were located. Some exhibits lined the perimeter, and at the foot of the four-story staircase, a koi pond rippled beside a padded ledge. Several couches broke the expanse, and the area vibrated with peaceful activity. A chubby preteen was sprawled on the banquette, where he remained for an hour, reading and making notes. A woman sat down and picked up some literature. A middle-aged couple canoodled together reading the exhibition catalog. A man with a goatee sat on the padded ledge around the koi, sketching. A woman waited for a companion to come out of the restroom. Everyone has his or her reasons for sitting down, but one fact underlies this scenario: the longer visitors sit, the stronger the bond with the museum.

If it's true, as museum researcher Beverly Serrell (1996) says, that the average visitor spends only twenty minutes per visit, then seating takes on greater importance. To engage visitors more fully, to encourage conversation and shared experience, and to revive sagging interest and bodies, you will have to provide chairs.

Seating is described by Paco Underhill, an indefatigable observer of human behavior, as an "active part of an exhibition," a place for reflection and reading relevant support material, a locus for discussion and "circular . . . conversation" (quoted in Black 2005, 87–88).

People who are sitting down look at other people, and this, too, enriches their visit; Elaine Heumann Gurion, a museum consultant who has studied public places and private intimidation, stresses the importance of scoping out one's fellow visitors in order to learn basic protocol such as the appropriateness of talking. Many visitors, not just new ones, feel strange in a museum and often intimidated. Research reveals that many people assume that everyone else inside is smarter and more sophisticated, and they need the reassurance of seeing people who look and act like they do.

ADVANTAGES IN STICKING AROUND

An analogy to this stop-and-sit behavior is the "stickiness" beloved by Web marketers, which claims that the longer one stays at a site, whether reading or clicking through, the better the awareness and probability of purchase. The "sticky" features of a website, especially the fun, interactive ones, have their parallel in the chairs, and design details like a fish pond that keep visitors sticking around pleasantly just a little while longer. When they do, resting before leaving, waiting for a friend to begin the visit, or reading your brochure, they are thinking about their visit. Many other connections fall into place as they discuss what they've seen with a friend, read up on the exhibits current and future, or look around and assess the distinctive features of their chosen destination.

And what about those sturdy souls who don't sit down? In the less desirable scenarios, they are rushing to leave, haven't spent enough time to get foot sore, and haven't socialized the experience with a companion. Older people who don't sit down present a scary yet preventable situation: perhaps the seats were too low for them to ease themselves into.

The importance of chairs was discovered some years ago by retail consumer researcher Paco Underhill, who noticed that men paced fretfully while their wives shopped and that, therefore, the women didn't buy as much as they might have. Underhill advised his client, Nordstrom, to add comfortable chairs for the men so that they could rest or snooze and leave the women free to spend. Indeed, one museum store now has the "man chairs" mentioned in chapter 2.

Take fifteen to thirty minutes to observe chair behavior and many striking yet obvious behaviors emerge. The most surprising is how many women use a seat as a place to put their handbags while they rummage for a pair of glasses, a tissue, or keys. Men use the seats for their coats while they're putting on other outerwear. A few, though not many, telephoners are relaxing into cell phone conversations. At one padded bench, near the museum's entrance, several people simply stood as if this piece of furniture marked the waiting area. It doesn't matter how people utilize a chair, bench, banquette, or couch; the significance is that while they are gathered there, they are extending their visit. While all marketers know the value of holding on to an existing customer, they may not realize that a chair holds on to a customer remarkably well.

With all that is riding on the chair, it's distressing to see how few people use one. In one thirty-minute observation of one museum lobby, more than sixty people entered, exited, or transited through the area, but fewer than half sat down. At the main entrance, where hundreds passed through, maybe ten actually sat down. At the museum with the koi pond and its padded ledge, many people sit to watch the fish as well as to relax and reflect. But at several museums, the benches at the video installations that serve as introductions get very few takers. At the tables overlooking the rose garden at a major botanical garden, very few people are enjoying the shade. At the exhibition of recycled materials repurposed into seats, hardly anyone accepts the guide's invitation to sit down. Even at the Cantigny complex of museums in Naperville, Illinois, where throughout its peaceful grounds banners depicting the benches on those selfsame grounds waved from lampposts, nobody was on the benches.

SEATS OF THE WORLD

Two of the best seats I've seen were at the Norton Museum of Art in West Palm Beach, Florida, and the Shanghai Museum of Contemporary Art. At the Norton, in the circular galley devoted to a ceiling installation of a Dale Chihuly glass sculpture, there are benches surrounding the perimeter of the room. The benches have no backs, just wavy surfaces. People lie on their backs to view the ceiling and then, remarkably, start talking to each other. It has the camaraderie and memory building of a sleepover. In Shanghai, in a 2008 retrospective of Ferragamo shoes, the room at the end of the tour was furnished with flat-screen monitors and giant-sized red plush pumps, and you'd better believe that everyone wanted to stretch out inside the shoes and watch the video.

Other seating arrangements encourage learning. Many museums now have reading areas in the galleries, sometimes no more than a table with a few chairs, where visitors can rest and get some background information. Others have classroom-type chairs throughout, complete with notepad (with logo) and a pencil. A major Southwest art museum themed its chairs with the galleries, painted wood in some and cushy armchairs in others. The Whitney Museum of American Art in New York has seats carved into the landings of its staircase and niches for exhibits, rendering the climb educational. In California, a major museum has a reading room, complete with bookshelves. The Musée du quai Branly in Paris has seats built into the walls next to small-screen monitors with videos that explicate the many aspects of this Museum of Man. At the Contemporary Art Museum in St. Louis, a noncollecting museum whose shows change about every four months, the Teaching Gallery has beanbag chairs. In Nauvoo, Illinois, where the Church of Latter-Day Saints operates a sophisticated living history museum, you must walk a distance to meet the ox-drawn wagon tour but can sit on benches while waiting; the costumed women who volunteer as guides as part of their mission will stroll over and chat about topics like apron patterns and butter churns. At the Museum of Contemporary Art in Chicago, there are cushiony sofas in the bookstore, and people do spend a lot of time there reading. At the Salt Lake City Public Library, which conducts museum-like tours of its striking new building, the children's department has nooks with multilevel seating for adults willing to bend over to get through the arched entry to these reading caves.

Some seats encourage reflection. The Tate Modern in London ranges benches along the windows overlooking the Thames River, a smart use of a good view that is echoed on comfortable seats in museums from Melbourne to Davenport, Iowa. At the De Young Museum in San Francisco, big squarish chunks of rough-hewn rock dot the courtyard, like the rest of this architecturally inventive destination a bridge between the natural world outside and artifacts within. For pure reflection, the Pulitzer Foundation rules, with a terrace accessible through a glass partition; there a seat has been carved into a huge boulder, and one can gaze at the reflecting pool.

Sometimes we learn from little children. At the First Division Museum on the grounds of General Robert L. McCormick's Catigny estate, children were stretched out on benches under the time line of World War I, the better to read along its entire length.

What all these museums all have—and it has nothing to do with size or interior design budget—is something to look at and distinctive places to sit while enjoying the view. And that's where your internal focus group should focus. Think about seats that provide sight lines and guide the discussion as discussed in the next paragraph.

DRILL-DOWN

If you delight at seeing visitors read your catalog, jump from their seats to embrace friends and sketch your exhibits; if, in short, you like nurturing your guests and reinforcing their goodwill, then take a seat and start brainstorming how you might get your visitors to sit down and stay a while. It's fun research because you start at home with your own staff and research the chair experience each one of them has had in museums or other places.

Here is a discussion guide:

Location: Where in our museum do we want people to spend five more minutes?

Space: How big a seat could we fit there? For example, is there space for a couch, a chair, or a beanbag?

Style: How could we make that seat interesting? Fun? Comfy? Useful?

View: What could we install near the seat that is interesting to gaze at?

Learning: Is there a learning experience we could introduce to our seating area (e.g., a chair with video monitor or outdoor bench near a petting zoo)?

Entertainment: How could we make the seating area more fun? One of the best seating gimmicks was a children's tour guide who plopped down on the floor in the middle of the lobby, encouraging all twenty of her charges to do the same.

Socialization: How could we bring people together in our seating area?

Branding: What kind of seating would reinforce our brand personality?

Memory: What kind of seats would help people remember us?

Status: For all those people we want to specially honor—members, trustees, media, and guest speakers—what kind of chairs should we set out?

Children: They need their creature comforts, and they're very adaptable. What can we learn about seating from them?

Other arts venues: What other arts activities do you participate in where you've experienced good seating? The Chicago Symphony has cushioned alcove seats built under the fan windows overlooking the showy second-floor lobby. Goodman Theatre, in Chicago, stretches benches along one wall of windows where you can wait for companions or talk during intermission. The Teatro Nacional de Costa Rica has foot rails in every row of its beautiful theater, which people under five feet four inches must surely applaud.

With such tangible and movable changes to your operation, one further kind of research is suggested: trial. Experiment with some new seating options and compare the before and after counts.

5

Turning Right

Disembarking from the escalators at the circular Hirshhorn Museum and Sculpture Garden in Washington, D.C., visitors confront a choice more confounding than most would believe unless it were pointed out to them: whether to turn left or right. To watch trying to choose between clockwise and counterclockwise is to see a pantomime of Marceauian intricacy: they turn right, then left; they point their index finger to the east, then west; they gesture to companions and stand one hand on hip, the other scratching their forehead. Sometimes they start out clockwise, come back to six o'clock, and turn counterclockwise. Ask the guards which way most people circulate, and they probably won't know or, more likely, have never thought to count. There are many phenomena occurring in museums that never make it onto a visitor questionnaire or focus group checklist yet that are so egregious and fraught with human nature and its marketing implications that they must be addressed. That is the value of observational research. The truth is that on one day at the Hirshhorn, 60 percent of all visitors opted to turn right, moving counterclockwise around the gallery.

This observation was tested again at the Museum of Contemporary Art in Chicago at an exhibition of works from the museum's collection. Visitors approached the exhibition area with a very clear choice of whether to start in the right-hand South Gallery or the North Gallery to the left. The wall outside the right-hand gallery contained the didactic panel for the show; standing in front of the wall outside the North (left-hand) Gallery was an interesting sculptural work. Most visitors eventually turned right, toward the introductory panel that clearly indicated the beginning of the show, but the decision-making process was painful. First, they walked toward the sculpture, then toward the panel. Many would go back to the sculpture and, finally, as if drawn by magnetic pull, to the right and the entrance to the museum. This same back-and-forth decision was also made, more deliberately, by a visitor in a wheelchair. The study of traffic flow is important to an exhibition because the curator has planned it with a purpose, and it has been designed to that goal. At both the Hirshhorn and Museum of Contemporary Art, the left-hand vista showed a very interesting piece of art—larger, more complex, and apparently more compelling than the work down the right-hand path. Yet on thinking it over, most visitors turned right anyway.

IN THE STORE

Right turns rule in the museum store as well. At the San Francisco Museum of Modern Art, virtually every shopper turned right around the long, rectangular display case. And they pretty much stayed right through the large store, invariably coming out on the left side. And while it might be supposed that people, like water, circle the drain in the opposite direction "down under," at the Art Gallery of New South Wales in Sydney, Australia, store shoppers swerved right as if they were avoiding a traffic cop.

Traffic flow occupies the mind of any business that has a lot of pedestrian traffic because moving people logically also moves them emotionally, and the direction of that flow affects many aspects of their operation: placement of benches, siting of signs, deployment of guards, as well as the essential business of where best to display the goods and install the cash register. At the store of the Chicago Botanic Garden, shoppers follow the postulated path and turn right at the entrance, emerging many minutes later to exit on the left side. A new configuration moved the checkout counter and cash register away from the left side of the entrance/exit to a spot halfway down the right-hand aisle. This right-minded placement also brilliantly catches shoppers in the first blush of their enthusiasm, on their rightward progression through the store. As museums today reinvestigate how high to hang a painting or whether to put the labels next to the work or at the end of the wall, the inclination of visitors becomes more significant.

LEFTIES AND RIGHTIES

And this information can't be gained from a focus group or survey. Ask folks gathered in a conference room which way they turn in a museum, and they probably wouldn't know. They could reconstruct their last visit and figure out which way they turned but would never realize how much physical and mental importance was invested in that maneuver. Some people will lift their finger and indicate a little circle. At this point, by the way, it would seem instructive to note whether they drew circles with their left or right hand, but this wouldn't matter. Lefties make up only 7 to 10 percent of the world's population, according to Chris McManus (2002), who wrote the definitive book on handedness; as many as 26 percent are left footed, it turns out, but left favoring or right, fully 60 to 80 percent turn counterclockwise.

In another proof of this phenomenon, consider the path taken by visitors to the Denver Art Museum's new addition, designed by Daniel Libeskind. This famously zigzag design has walls that meet at disconcerting angles and a maze-like appearance that daunts everyone when they first enter the wing. According to the guards, every single visitor turns right immediately. Although they will soon get confused by the unprecedented layout, they automatically go the comfortable way—right—before turning to their inner GPS and zigzagging through the gallery.

Because so much of a museum's layout depends on traffic flow—galleries, store, restaurant, lecture halls, and queues—it pays to refine the methodology of this research. Sometimes observational research results in no more than a mind-boggling revelation, and that's enough to get the brainstorming started. On the right–left subject, more work is needed. Observations should be made at all times of day, on all days of the week, and in different seasons of the year. Holidays might make a difference. Museums with a greater dependence on tourism might pay special attention to heavy tourist attractions. On the same note, local people might be so familiar with the museum that to change an accustomed route would be confusing.

The right–left phenomenon is important, and there is a "universal human desire to treat left and right as symbolically different," according to McManus (2002). In most Western cultures, right is good and left not so. In a *New Yorker* article on children's calculacy, or number literacy, a study found that children counted by pointing to objects with their right-hand digits (Holt

2008). When the hands were crossed, with the left hand on the right side, they pointed with the left hand.

TRAFFIC JAMS IN THE CAFETERIA

You might wonder if, on another day, in another museum space, the same rule applies. It does. The lunchtime cafeteria customers at a large art museum could be observed crowding into the right-hand line. In fact, the inclination was so strong that although the right-hand line had the more expensive offering—a roast beef carvery—and only one server, everyone turned right anyway. Over on the left side, there was no wait for the less expensive pizza and two employees standing around with nothing to do. In this case, making the right turn was a wrong move for visitor and museum alike, leading to customer dissatisfaction, employee disgruntlement, misallocation of resources, and possibly some stale food.

IMPLICATIONS

Implications of the counterclockwise preference touch every aspect of the museum experience and hence the marketing. Good marketing means, first and foremost, retaining the interest and loyalty of existing customers, and if that includes catering to penchants like right-hand turns, so be it. Exhibitions themselves and their layouts can be planned more coherently and informatively to retain the interest of visitors. Design of other spaces, such as the museum store and cafeteria, will definitely benefit from humans' seemingly skeletal imperative to veer right. When you know where visitors will go first, you can deploy your guards better and place more information desks there. You can route docent tours more effectively and situate the audio handset counter more efficiently.

DRILL-DOWN

Further research includes corroborating for yourself this phenomenon, and reviewing at all the byways and crossroads in your institution. Larger museums, botanic and zoological gardens, and living museums especially might want to look beyond their galleries, cafés, and stores to help visitors cover larger territory. Observe how they steer to and through the lobby, information area, and tour staging area. Follow them to the theater, education rooms, research spaces, and event facilities. Look at the signage on walking paths, vehicle routes, and parking lots. Considerable energy goes into navigating a museum, and you can ease the path.

Don't even think about calling in architects and environmental designers, at least not yet. You can explore the implications and further action in-house by sitting down in small groups and brainstorming. If this process seems overwhelming, make the acquaintance of what industry terms a "skunkwork project." When an organization of any size wants to think way outside the box, without fear of failing, a small task force is assigned to develop a trial program, in this case new right-turning traffic paths. Everyone understands that the project is experimental and that no one will be judged harshly if it ends up not smelling so sweet. It's research of the highest order, a rather brave foray into the little known. Your task force should meet regularly, but the schedule needn't be rigid. You can budget funds for more extensive trials, but you can try out ideas on a shoestring. What's important is that new schemes are articulated and tried, that valid insights are given a chance to be judged.

Marketers are always adapting to the needs of the customers they already have and to the consumer they hope to get. The same mind-set that develops improved products, creates promotions and methods of distribution, and communicates through evolving media can also be applied to that large and limitless entity: visitor services.

6

Dress Code

On Friday noon at the Nelson-Atkins Museum of Art in Kansas City, Missouri, as people walked down the sunlit ramp of the celebrated new wing, it appeared that a special event was taking place. Many women were in high heels. But the well-shod feet continued their walk over to the popular dining room, an upscale cafeteria, and from there throughout the galleries. Suffice to say that there were hardly any torn jeans or running shoes. Even older women wore little heels. Even younger women wore jackets and blouses. Men wore suits, jackets, or prep-correct sweaters and pressed shirts. Granted, many variables could explain this observation. It was a weekday, so one wouldn't expect a teen or young adult crowd. It was just before noon, so there could have been a board meeting taking place elsewhere in the museum. But the observation is significant because it holds true in other large-city art museums where, regardless of age or fashion orientation, the crowds dress for show. One can see heeled boots, short skirts, and colorful scarves on the women and jackets or neat sweaters on the men, a general look of finery adding visual appeal to the exhibits all around. Visits to other art museums corroborated the observation that, when it comes to art museums, visitors like to be seen as well as to see.

It would seem that museums visitors expect to be seen. After all, for an hour of more of activity, they want to—or are required to—shed their coats. In addition, as has been discussed in studies of visitor experiences, people consider museums a socializing experience, a place to meet friends or entertain out-of-towners.

The other rationales for this museum dress code are intriguing. Museums have restaurants, and restaurants are places where women are accustomed to dressing up and men encouraged to wear something nice. As in the rest of the museum, the lights are always on, another reason to look good. All this underlines the reality that museums are destinations, a way of positioning your product that is growing in favor.

This brings us to a comparison with your competition, namely, other arts venues, such as theaters, concert halls, and lecture spaces.

PART OF THE EXPERIENCE

The museum experience is much more than a cliché in a mission statement or manual; rather, it is a palpable event where the experiencers are part of the show. Museum visitors walk around, go back, stop longer at one exhibit, and bypass another altogether. They jump in and participate and dress the part. The human spirit reacts one way when it can enter a museum at any time, take a guided tour or not, duck into the museum store, or take a time out at a café. The individual feels kind of carefree. The human mind acts differently when it must follow a schedule of curtain time, sit in a dark room for an hour at a time, adhere to the length of intermission, and remember to turn off a cell phone or risk the ridicule of several hundred strangers. In this situation, the individual is restricted to group strictures. It is no quirk that folks in a museum talk to each other, while audiences in a theater stay silent. And the emotional aspect of dress reflects each experience.

Compared to the verbal arts, visual arts venues such as museums lead in the splendor of their attendees. At the theater, specifically at weekday evening performances, the dress code is "day-end dreary." To start with the feet, frankly the least intrusive way to observe a stranger, one will see sturdy walking shoes that look scuffed and trail worn. Further scanning reveals yeoman-like coats, drab slacks, and nondescript tops, unrelieved by scarves, jewelry, or other frippery. The men seem similarly dressed: appropriate but dull. When it comes to theater, it seems, the play's the thing.

At the symphony, people dress well, perhaps in deference to the high ticket prices, partly as a reflection of the older age of symphony-goers, and yet the garb is dark and sedate. Picture the "sea of faces" in a cliché symphony audience photograph; you can hardly see what the people are wearing, and maybe that explains everything.

On Sunday afternoon, older people make a day of theater and concert outings, and the women are cheerfully dressed. Likewise, at Friday afternoon Chicago Symphony matinees, the crowd is mostly older women. The restaurant is open for preperformance donor dining, and fashion plays first chair. The women look smashing because, as one doyenne put it, her peers, many of them widows, don't have many other opportunities to dress up. Scale this scenario down for smaller cities with smaller theater seasons, and the concept holds: older women like to dress up once in a while, and the theater provides the social opportunity to do so.

Operas are a different story. This verbal-visual art form attracts a peacock audience of color and fashion statement. Perhaps because operas have long intermissions, one can view a parade of elegance, showiness, and sometimes foolishness, a delightful spectacle that supplements the grand scene onstage.

An important addition to the arts scene is the lecture, now a standard part of museum, theater, and music offerings and a growing profit center in municipal humanities programs. The lecture audience is thought provoking because it looks so different. In addition to a wide range of ages, lectures attract people who aren't shy about coming alone. Lecture audiences tend to talk to each other, and not just in the lobby but long after and in meaningful terms. Whereas theater- or museumgoers will sum up a performance with "wasn't it marvelous?" or "I just loved it," lecture-goers will comment on specific ideas. Interestingly, people at lectures dress brightly. You can count the number of colorful scarves and jewelry on the women and the natty sweaters on the men. This is an occasion loaded with creative thinking and social interaction; the dress code correlates.

To gain insights, sometimes it helps to look across borders and to competitive leisure activities. In São Paulo, Brazil, the shopping malls are practically a cultural imperative. They are gated and exclusive, with fine stores and wealthy shoppers. There's crime outside the gates, but inside security prevails. Here people come to look and meet: it's an acknowledged place to meet the opposite sex. And the young people dress for it. Museums serve a similar purpose, as with the Friday night cheese-and-wine events, and might present similar opportunities throughout the week.

Why should this matter when nobody fixates anymore on the way people should dress and many pretend not to care? Long gone are the days when, at Chicago's Museum of Science and Industry, a little girl who showed up in pants had to wrap a museum-provided nylon skirt around her waist. Point in fact: people do care, and visitors to museums seem to care a lot. Time and time again, on different days of the week and at different institutions, visitors are flaunting it.

VISITOR BELIEF SYSTEMS

How people dress is, of course, one manifestation of their values and beliefs. Museums will eternally compete with other arts organizations for the long-term loyalty of arts enthusiasts who believe in a given arts venue. And museums have a lot of advantages that help them compete: lower to nonexistent ticket prices, no constraining schedules, generous hours of operation (including some evenings), room to move about and interact with other people and the exhibits, interpretation on various levels, light, freedom to talk and share, full exposure to other devotees, and—key to this chapter's thesis—a predisposition to being visibly, tangibly part of the whole.

The museum visitor—woman or man, older or younger, richer or poorer—dresses for the occasion. The implications for the museum reach into every corner of operations—curatorial, education, facilities rental, marketing, membership, and development—from the accessibility of the coatroom to mirrors in the store, because your customers are also exhibits, and they need to be preserved and displayed to their best advantage.

Visitors come to museums to socialize, interact, and enrich their minds, and they expect to be seen and appreciated. Obvious first responses to these needs are provisions for a fast-moving coat check, lounges with mirrors, and at least a few areas that are well lit.

These visitors plan to spend some time with you, so you need well-spaced benches or other seating, some of which might be in a snack lounge or café. Dressed-for-the-visit visitors want to be seen and to see others because they are here, many of them, in a social role, so there must be public spaces with good sight lines. They wear pretty things and hope to find more pretty things in the store. This is not to eschew education, learning, and scholarly endeavor, but it's important to recognize that dressing well and learning well are not mutually exclusive.

GUIDE TO LEARNING STYLES

Educators have always grappled with tools to aid learning, and it's worth asking if the way people dress offers clues to their learning styles. Certainly, individuality in dress reminds us that people also learn in individual ways: some read labels, some look at the visuals, some need to talk it over with friends, and some need to listen to docents. Museums have the unique combination of visual, spatial, verbal, and aural expression to appeal to all learners, and it's time to mix and match those expressions to satisfy everyone. Curators, as they select and display works, have rare power to dress the galleries, to appeal to all kind of learners and enjoyers. The intensity and range of individual expression is enthralling in its possibilities: here are visitors engaged enough to join the visual display, engaged enough to absorb in different ways what you have to show.

The social aspects of dressing well bode well for the social spaces in museums and the growing importance of facilities rental. Individuals and groups clearly view museums as gathering places, so it's not a leap to envision the museum as a place for book clubs, office parties, and birthday celebrations; there's a panorama of get-togethers beyond blowout events like weddings and charity galas. This is an easy extension of current thinking, especially for smaller museums.

As for internal congregating, membership building could use more physical contact and less e-mail or letters. Visitors get their bearings in a new museum by observing others, and newcomers especially look to those they perceive as more experienced to show them how to act. It's essential to reassure visitors that they belong, or they'll never return, let alone sign up for membership. Membership implies belonging to a group that resembles one's own tastes and standards; to become a member, one measures not only the objects in a museum but the other members as well to ascertain how their own taste and standards fit in. This applies to any of the arts—theater, opera, symphony, or dance—but museums have an advantage above all the others because it is so easy for the casual visitor to see and interact with both the show and the people who participate in it. Dress styles—whether showy or elegant, simple or uncaring—are a code, a symbol of how regular museumgoers view a given museum. For new visitors or ones who want to get more involved, one way to figure out what institutions are like is to evaluate the regulars, and dress certainly helps unlock the code. When new volunteers or board members are being courted, it's understood they'll assess the current group and, con-sciously or unconsciously, make judgments on the basis of appearance and dress. Notice how people dress for your institution—not to judge them but to get a sense of who they are and what they need from you.

ACTIVE AND ENGAGED

Here's an important group to observe, and their dress indicators tell you a lot. Dress matters greatly to the over-55 age category, which is visible at the end of standard surveys and growing more visible every day. This is a group that no longer can be casually dismissed. This market segment has resources, health, education, and a set of role models quite different from what it had a generation ago. The knee-jerk image of a granny in an apron or gramps in overalls is funny but all too true (what comes to your mind first?) and all too false. Realize that today's grandparents now work full time, ski, chauffeur grandchildren, and travel the world, and that you must weave them into your business plan in a different way. Start by looking at them in your galleries. They dress well because they are vital and engaged, and your programs are important in their active lives.

Another new reality is the infusion of visitors from every country of the world. A big-city museum docent who keeps track of the countries has come face-to-face with China, Bulgaria, Singapore, Colombia, Brazil, Kenya, Iran, and Turkey, among others. Although there is no reliable information on how other cultures dress for museums, we can assume that such visits matter to them and that they will dress appropriately. When you see them dressed well, you appreciate the respect they feel.

Finally, there is word of mouth. For you to sustain success, your visitors must help you spread the message. Consciously or unconsciously, part of their remembered experience will be the look of the other visitors around them. This is not to promote dressing up or dressing brightly. Many of your visitors will be more comfortable looking at young people in jeans or old people in comfortable shoes. The trick is to ascertain the many different types of visitors you have, and dress code observations will help you segment your market.

Details, such as heel height or the color of scarf, might seem small, but larger theories are made of such details. Steven D. Levitt, the iconoclastic social economist, compares it to looking at the world through a straw, the objective being to scrutinize everyday habits in ways they haven't been considered before (Levitt and Dubner 2005). Or, as Dan Ariely (2008) teaches in his new book on consumer behavior, after you've heard a story about people's behavior in one situation, stop and consider what it means for you.

DRILL-DOWN

You may think, "Not many people dress up in our museum," but if just a few do, it's worth pursuing those individuals, whom some organization and behavior researchers call "positive deviants." There is always a small minority in any group or community who acts differently from the norm and seems to thrive anyway. Research that learns from what the successful minority do has been applied to every social situation from undernourished Vietnamese villagers to corporations undergoing change, and you can apply it to your museum. If you assemble a focus group, says Jerry Sternin (2009), the leading advocate for positive deviants, try to get a group of like-minded people together so that they can share their common behavior. This is not a time to bring in a diverse group for a brainstorming session but an occasion to drill more deeply into their shared behavior.

Think about how people act, don't expect them to act on how you think: that's the thinking proclaimed by change experts, the people who study things like positive deviance. You can study it with one small focus group. Ideally, you will gather people who actually do dress especially colorfully or carefully; you can identify them at the time of a visit and sign them up for a future focus group. You could also assemble any group of women with a fair amount of certainty that they will be talkative and informative about clothes.

Start with general questions about how they dress and then focus in on specifics:

How do you dress for a visit to a museum?

Does it vary by museum type?

How much time do you usually spend at a museum? Does that affect how you dress?

How do you dress when you're out of town and sightseeing? Does that change how you would dress for a museum visit?

How do your friends dress? What do you think motivates them?

Do you look at other people at museums? Describe them.

Thinking of the following kinds of museum visitors, how would you define them?

Female wearing pants and sweater

Female wearing a pantsuit

Female wearing a skirt

Female in little heels

Female with a coat on

Female wearing walking sandals

Female with interesting scarf or jewelry

Female in jeans and T-shirt

Female in dress and high heels

Male in khaki pants and shirt

Male wearing sport coat

Male in sturdy shoes

Male wearing a suit and tie

Male in jeans and T-shirt

Obviously, you will gear these questions to your geography, climate, and culture. Also ask the following:

Who accompanies you on a museum visit? What do they wear?

We've noticed that a lot of women *not* wearing typical walking shoes in the museum. Sometimes they even wear little heels. What do you think of that?

What other cultural activities do you or your friends participate in? Do you go to plays, concerts, the symphony or opera, or lectures?

How do you dress for them? Is it different from what you wear to museums?

Here are some items from our museum store. What would you select to wear the next time you visit us? (If you don't have a store, borrow items from a local retailer.)

Of course, after each question, follow up with "why?" None of these questions are designed to provide your marketers with solid demographics or solutions to problems. They are meant help the participants relive how people actually act, to provoke their thoughts and start their conversation, and, ultimately, to provide new insights for you.

If you don't assemble a focus group, you can ask a short form of these questions in a written questionnaire distributed at the admissions counter or on a laptop at the coat check.

People dress for themselves and others, they dress for the occasion and to make the occasion ever better, and they dress up because it is fun and makes them feel good. Peacocks strut, and so do people, and the implications behind all those rituals are worth studying further.

7

Museumgoers Don't Get Fat: Tribal Marketing

A subset of the well-dressed museumgoer is the fit-and-trim museumgoer. This unsuspected observation was made at the National Museum of Victoria/ Australia, itself a sleek piece of architecture in Melbourne's Federation Square. It houses art by Australian artists of all generations and genres, and while the displayed works come in all shapes and sizes, no visitors enter who are over-weight. The stream of people looked like the Olympics opening ceremony: everyone was trim and fit. In thirty minutes, there were only three visitors who could be termed heavy, and the two categories of visitors had to be redefined as rail thin and average. Could it be that overweight people don't go to museums? Or do art and slimness go together? Is there some fitness club requirement?

This seems a dangerously narrow characterization, even politically incorrect, but it is a good example of the new discipline of tribal marketing and therefore is worth exploring further. Marketers are embracing so-called tribal segments, in which audiences are understood by their shared lifestyles and pastimes rather than demographics or even psychographics because it helps communicate with them individually. Personalized communication is the way the marketing world is headed, thanks to the Internet. It's the basis of social marketing and the new digital media. So grouping museum audiences by lifestyle doesn't seem inappro-priate. The trend in Australia was clear and fruitful enough to prompt further observations at many museums in the United States. The observation held true at museums across the spectrum; unweighty museum visitors are a global tribe.

The concept of global tribes, a ten-year-old concept that's gaining currency now, started as so many new consumer patterns did: with the Internet. Now that the world's consumers have settled into daily Internet usage, they find new ways to connect with their purchase preferences and with each other. User groups were just the beginning. Mobile devices, fashion, cars, entertainment, and eBay all are global, and rituals from listening to music to auctioning jewelry bring people of different nations, ages, and backgrounds together. Marketers now have narrow but large segments of consumers to draw from. They don't need to sell to everybody—the old-style mass marketing—because the sliver groups, global in composition, are large. Digital marketers can reach these new groupings through their lifestyles, and it's a boon to have a target that is so clearly defined.

SHARED RITUALS

Listen to how one arts expert describes a tribal segment. Conductor and composer Esa-Pekka Salonen (2008) talks about his affinity with other French horn players. It's such a horribly hard instrument to play, he says, that "French horn players globally all support each other . . . we end up drinking beer together after the performance." Note that this is not simply a general-ized group of educated men but a group of guys who play a difficult musical instrument. And a marketer doesn't need a special interest magazine or an expensive mailing list for this target. The Internet is very efficient. Think about the tribes within a museum's target audience; it's a whole new way to reframe customer experience.

Fitness as a ritual, it turns out, might well be an indicator of museum audiences. In researching creative people and the "creative class," Richard Florida (2004) ranked fifty American cities for their fitness, measured by readily available statistics such as daily exercise, obesity, and smoking. He then ranked cities for various creative attributes, such as number of arts and research organizations, and concluded that the twenty fittest cities were also the leading "creative centers" (his term), such as San Diego, Minneapolis, Seattle, Washington, D.C., and San Francisco.

IMPLICATIONS

There is no evidence that museums should cater to people who exercise and watch their diets. However, there is evidence that museumgoers have other lifestyle habits in common besides their fondness for museums (slimness is only one) that we should know about and that can be found by looking at their "tribal" groups, not demographic ones. Some educated guesses about the habits and rituals of the slim-and-fit tribe follow:

They spend a lot of their leisure time in fitness activities like walking, gym workouts, or sports. That's leisure competition you might not have factored in when looking at leisure activities that compete for your fit-and-trim customers' time and money.

In warm weather, they stay outside a lot, maybe more than you planned when estimating summer attendance.

They're accustomed to following regimens and probably move through your museum quickly and thoroughly. Give them plenty to see.

Perhaps they schedule museum time like they do court time or gym time—by the hour. Are your docent tours aware that everybody moves faster now?

Some of their leisure money goes to adventure vacations or gear, which are relatively expensive hobbies. They spend generously for their leisure and that might include museums.

Your survey questions on household income might be misleading. People buy what they want and compensate in other areas to pay for it. People who weigh their calories and balance their workout schedules are good at balancing their leisure dollars.

Fit-and-trims will be healthy and vibrant well into their older years, so don't underestimate them as visitors, donors, and volunteers. Don't clump them in your mind with the vague 65-plus group as most surveys do.

Review your restaurant menu.

DRILL-DOWN

To further explore the relationship between your museum and the peculiar interests of the fit-and-trim tribe, schedule a two-hour meeting for guided discussions with a team of stakeholders selected from every area of the institution. The goal: finding benefits within your institution that appeal to the Fit-and-Trim tribe. This kind of research applies to any tribal group you want to target.

To ensure audacious thinking, assemble a team of rivals. The concept is borrowed from Doris Kearns Goodwin's (2006) book about Lincoln's cabinet, which was composed of the men he ran against for the nomination to the presidency. They were different people with one major interest in common—the country—and they found common ground. The model is replicated frequently by corporate task forces that are assembled from every corner of the organization. Form your discussion group from administration, curatorial, collections, education, marketing, and Web designers as well as board members, volunteers, docents, and guards—one of each. Mix older, experienced people with new hires. An ideal group is six to eight people. Change the individual members as needed, but don't try for consensus. You want a stew of new ideas. One or two meetings will get things bubbling.

Here's a discussion guideline: start with each member of the group describing his or her own tasks within the museum. This breaks the ice and, in larger museums, serves as a primer on how the museum operates. Next discussion point: what works in your daily job? This is positive and gets everyone thinking about the museum's systems. This is what visitors see.

Now get edgy and ask everyone to contribute something that went wrong, preferably amusing, in the past week. It's amazing how wonderful pearls grow from little specks of annoyance. Emphasize easily solved problems; these, too, are what visitors see.

With the personal experiences and incidents you've collected, you're ready to speculate on how each relates to a given tribe's experiences. With three dozen or so institutional pieces to toss around, conjecture where energetic people would fit in. Think where on your website you'd link to a fitness interest. It's a mix-and-match jigsaw puzzle that forces unusual connections. Most of the combinations won't fit, and many will be ridiculous. But like trial and error with a puzzle, some combinations of visitor motivation and museum operation will dovetail. At that "aha" moment, your research has done its job.

You can use this kind of internal ideation session to rethink any problem or opportunity at the museum. Its rather unruly format works perfectly for a project that intends to break some rules. And when you decide to slice your target audience differently and take into account tribal preferences, you are definitely breaking some old rules.

8

Men: A New Market Segment

Years ago, I overheard a conversation between a couple lunching at a history museum café. The details weren't audible, but the intellectual energy was clear. She'd say something, and he'd finish the sentence; he'd start a comment, and she'd finish it. How delightful, I thought, a real fifty-fifty relationship. Ever since, I have noticed that about 50 percent of all museum visitors are men. A docent at an art museum confirms that about half the people taking tours are men. On successive afternoons at a large metropolitan art museum, 30 to 50 percent of the visitors were men. By the way, statistically, just over half of all scientists in the United States are men, and 62 percent of history PhDs in 2000 were men. See where I'm going?

Even knowing that half the population are men, marketers never give men the respect they should have as consumers. They come in all ages and styles, with their own attitudes and motivations, and each one reconfirms the premise that they deserve closer study, especially in museums.

Most men come to museums with women, and some appear to be dragged to the museum in the "yes, dear" mode, but many also appear to have individual motivations. There was the grandfather coping with the snowsuit of a child in a stroller, and there were men of all ages who came in alone. Of the young couples who enter a museum, in many cases it was the men who were taking the lead, striding into the lobby eager to show their girlfriends the sights. Several male twosomes walked purposefully, chatting, the way men might act walking into a conference room; they clearly knew their way around a museum. A small percentage of the male cohort was minorities. On a 1:30 P.M. observation, a few suits-and-ties men could be seen leaving, undoubtedly coming from a luncheon board meeting. There was a high percentage of older men and a low percentage of men who looked like tourists. In summary, all manner of men visit museums, and each slice of the segment merits marketing scrutiny.

A typical survey would miss the subtle differences and superficially categorize men only by their age, ZIP code, and possibly whether they were tourists. Perhaps the survey would identify other arts interests or where they had heard about the museum. But undiscovered by these surveys is the mélange of male habits, likes and dislikes, backgrounds and motivations. Too bad. Although millions of hours have been spent deciphering the motivations of women consumers, only a miniscule fraction of that has been spent understanding men, even though men are expected to share women's lives, interests, leisure activities, and family concerns. Many men could be the museum trip decision maker. They stand a good chance of being the ones who, before the visit, check online for directions and, once inside the lobby, unfold the map and plan the attack. Men chat up the guards for information, hang around the store while women shop, and pay for the lunch. All these men will carry away idiosyncratic impressions of your museum that will inform their future choices. And here's the caution: they may not be the ones to complete the on-site questionnaires. If you're missing the input of 50 percent of your visitors, look around and observe them all the more carefully; they're very interesting people.

IMPLICATIONS OF MEN IN THE ROOM

Underlying the number of male visitors is the quantity of purchasing decisions made by men and the skimpiness of museum activities that recognize this. If any museum reviewed the totality of its operation, it might find that men were undervalued. Look at the maleness of yours. Museums are in the business of selling not only learning and enrichment but also memberships and support. Look at not only the focus of your exhibitions but also the "quicheness" of café offerings, the tone of voice of your tours, and the features of store merchandise. Reread your membership materials and evaluate them for appeals to men; many of the awards for higher membership levels are of the tote-bag and store-discount variety. Consider how much of the promotional materials target or picture children; men like children as much as women do but aren't particularly motivated by them in advertising. Ask yourself if your ancillary programs—lectures and fund-raising events—are men friendly. How many of your programs are on evenings or weekends? Does your volunteer program—from recruitment to orientation to rewards—relate to men? Critique your promotional materials for male orientation because, even today, it's a marketing truism that most advertising is directed at women; analyze whether you unconsciously adhere to this dictum, too.

Now consider men as not only visitors but also community partners. While observing the male visitors to your galleries, put yourself in their shoes and walk with them back to their offices. These men are in the position of sponsoring an exhibition, hosting off-site museum lectures, talking up volunteerism to their employees, providing in-kind donations, and approving budgets for school field trips. Visitors have real lives and occupations in offices, stores, schools, and factories. This caveat also applies to women visitors.

Men are hunters, and women are gatherers, says Paco Underhill (2005), who studies consumer behavior at the retail level. If the genders shop differently at stores, be assured that they consume differently at museums.

Here are eleven ways that men customarily differ from women in habits and preferences that may affect your operations:

Interests: Men like spears and armor; women like the First Lady dresses. Men like vehicles; women like decorative arts.

Reading tolerance: Note how long women will stop to read a label and then time the men. Men like to get to the point; women meander.

Walking pace: Women tend to walk more slowly, and they don't mind detouring if something attracts them. Men usually have a goal and then move deliberately toward it. Women stop and start; men keep going.

Literature: Observation suggests that men are the ones who read the maps and floor plans, perhaps because women have at least a handbag on their arm and maybe a child as well. Men also seem to be the ones charged with holding and carrying the printed pieces.

Paying for or picking up the tickets at the front desk: Observation says that this is man's work.

Need to sit down: At the retail level, this is definitely a male habit. Observe how many men sit down in the galleries to look at the exhibits.

Asking questions: It depends on the nature of the question, whether it's for specific directions or general information. Women tend to ask functional questions at the information desk about tour times and café hours; men ask docents content questions about the exhibits. In the restaurant, women query the wait staff about the menu. During fund-raising solicitations, men quiz the solicitor about financials.

Fund-raising: Digressing from the physical museum to the institutional one, it would be useful to know who makes the philanthropic decisions and who writes the checks.

Shopping: Although men are thought to be genetically disinclined to shop, you'd be surprised by how many roam the store with their female companions.

Tours: Men might make up less than half of all museum visitors but fully half of most docent-led tours.

Technology: This broad category, encompassing touch screens, podcasts, individual audio wands, and other interactive interpretation tools, needs to be scrutinized with a fresh eye. With traditional interactive exhibits, many going back half a century, you can easily see male-versus-female usage, but recent innovations allow not only more choices but more user input as well. While men will explore technology longer than women, women may be more attracted to the lure of additional information.

Socialization: It is true that women talk on the phone and lunch with friends more than men, but it's a misreading of their overt socializing to assume that the taciturn man doesn't need companionship at the museum. Few men visit a museum solo, and they differ from their comrades who do.

DRILL-DOWN: TALK TO MEN
It's time to talk to men, and the first round of research is any easy one: talk to the men on your staff. If there are enough of them, assemble a focus group simply to uncover some issues. A premier use of focus groups is to open your

collective mind to a situation that's just starting to niggle at you. If you can't assemble a group of men, conduct some one-on-one conversations with any man you can find. If you have an all-woman staff, that fact underscores the elusiveness of the problem.

A focus group of five to ten people is the best way to unearth motivations and attitudes. In groups, men will develop ideas they might not conjecture on their own, and they'll hear the words that help them express those thoughts. With groups, the facilitator is able to follow through on an idea, to drill down without seeming to badger the individual. Once one idea is out on the table, others flow as each person articulates his own perspective.

A group of fewer than five men decreases the chances of diverse thoughts, and you want as wide a range of ideas as possible. Although researchers try to recruit participants within a certain geographic area or whose interests mesh with your type of museum, you might not have the luxury of such specificity in recruiting men. A smaller group also is susceptible to the dominance of one person. There's always a chance of a dominant personality taking the lead, talking too much, and arguing with the others. Men are considered a tougher focus group if only because they don't go to them very often and are unaccustomed to the process. Unlike women, men don't spend much time sitting around on couches talking to each other. Even in a business setting, men's roles are to discuss and come to a consensus or conclusion; the goal of focus groups is simply to air different points of views.

A group of more than ten men is unwieldy. While waiting for one person to comment, the other nine get restless. If two or more people contribute similar thoughts, it's easy for the others to feel outweighed and simply say, "I agree with them." With many ideas put forward, men might feel compelled to trump all the others when, in fact, it's perfectly acceptable in a focus group to agree with another person's thoughts.

Once you have a group of five to ten men, the structure of the conversation is similar to that of any focus group: start with introductions to put everyone at ease and general questions about leisure activities, and then quickly home in with questions about museums and specific probes about different aspects of your own museum. Keep the discussion moving with cross-examination of ideas that other participants have put forth. You don't need to ask man-specific questions unless the men volunteer them. You'll get man-specific answers.

Some questions to ask are the following:

What do you do for leisure?

How do you spend weekends?

Describe your last vacation.

We're here today to talk about men's attitudes towards museums. When was the last time you visited a museum? What kind of museum was it?

What surprised you about your museum visit?

What did you like best? What didn't you like about the museum?

What do you remember about school field trips to museums? What has changed?

Thinking of all your male acquaintances, friends, family, or work associates, who would you expect to enjoy museums and why? (It's often easier to get participants, especially men, to speculate about motivations when they concern other people.)

When you visit museums, do you shop or eat at the restaurant or café? Why or why not?

Do you ever attend lectures, performances, or fund-raising events at museums? What do you think about them?

Are men different from women when it comes to museumgoing behavior? How?

The men you know who enjoy museums: Describe their involvement.

What would prompt you to visit [name of your museum]? What would motivate you to go to any museum?

A current exhibition at [your museum] is [name of exhibition]. Does it sound interesting?

Would you take a guided tour or look on your own?

What would deter from visiting [name of museum]?

Expect to ask a lot of "whys" and "explain furthers." Men aren't as voluble as women, and you need to keep prompting. Place a mental space between your questions so that you can probe any answer immediately. For example, Jack said that he didn't like field trips as a child because he couldn't run around. Does anyone else feel that way? When you get a surprising or provocative response, drill down a little and uncover the attitude behind it. In addition, if you are confused by a response, clarify it at once; not only will it help you ask further questions, but it may help the rest of the group as well.

In other focus groups, you might spend more time probing attitudes toward your own museum. However, in this case you're interested mainly in the attitudes of men as distinct from women, and you must focus on that. Be very clear about the purpose of the focus group. These groups cost time and money, and you need to stay on the path. In addition, you don't want to confuse your group. Let them in on the reason for the focus group, and they'll work with you.

Try not to involve the men's families in your questions; you're trying to get each man's thoughts, not habits inculcated by his girlfriend, wife, mother, or children. Try not to use the pronouns "we" or "our." The facilitator or moderator is a neutral person whose role is to elicit thoughts and comments. Ideally, the moderator is not an employee and, in any case, must assure the group that he or she will be unbiased and unaffected by any answers.

Focus groups should last one to two hours. Have water or soft drinks available. Usually food is not offered, as it's a distraction, noisy, and messy. An exception might be made for men's groups, especially since they're usually held after work; hungry men won't be able to concentrate for long. If you do serve food, keep it light and put away the plates before you start talking.

Most focus groups pay a small stipend for participants' time and travel. Because men are harder to recruit, you should definitely be prepared to pay anywhere from $10 to $75, depending on your city and location. If you're recruiting professional men or specific segments like community leaders or audio engineers, the price goes up.

ONE-ON-ONE INTERVIEWS

Because a good man is hard to find, all you need is one to start the exploration. If you don't have the time, the money, or a conference room for a focus group, conduct some one-on-one interviews. The one-on-one interview is no substitute for the broader knowledge gained from a focus group and is usually used to clarify concepts tossed out in focus groups, but any information is better than none.

The advantage of this type of research is convenience. Rather than recruit through a professional research firm, start with any man you know. With a one-on-one interview, you can get to the point quickly. As with all research, new knowledge leads to more questions, so expect to follow up on any intriguing information. Unlike a focus group, you don't need to break the ice first. Start with a general introduction but hasten to the purpose of your research. Use the same questions as for a focus group and probe all the answers.

9

Lunchtime Stories

Guess who stays at the restaurant table longest? At the Milwaukee Art Museum café, on a bright March Sunday, five tables of diners were under observation: young parents with a seven-year-old boy; a jeans-wearing twenty-something couple; a well-dressed forty-something couple; a threesome of artsy-looking types, dressed for business; and two ladies of a certain age, burdened with tote bags. The answer to which group lingered over lunch is emblematic of why observational research is so valuable. You may be surprised to learn that it was the family with the child who sat the longest: fifty minutes. The group that dashed away quickest: the artsy types, who ate and ran in thirty-four minutes. The two ladies gabbed for only thirty-seven minutes. Both the younger couple who talked intensely and the older couple who chatted more perfunctorily enjoyed their meal for forty-four minutes.

Food achieves varying levels of importance, depending on museum size, budget, and location. If you have the budget for a café, the benefits are worth it. People eat for refreshment, sociability, relaxation, entertainment, and reflection, but "people" is too broad a term if you want to understand how they really enjoy your museum. Look at each of the five previously mentioned tables as market segments and heed the nonverbal table talk; you'll begin to uncover some new insights into your visitors.

The parents with the little boy obviously were enjoying the opportunity to be together, quietly, and although they were relaxing and refreshing like any other group, they probably appreciated the interlude more and for different reasons than you might imagine. Their little boy was entertaining himself, and they had precious weekend minutes that young parents don't often get. Parents of one child are apt to still be dual earners, and for members of that category of parent who take the kids with them everywhere, the museum becomes a destination for the two of them, not only an enriching must-see.

Of the other groups of visitors, other defining implications might be drawn. The young adults, who are usually boxed into the young, low-income demographic, actually fit the more desirable psychographic of people who like museums. Contented young couples are cause for celebration; museums need the blue jeans set if they are to survive, and, in fact, the restaurant was full of young people enjoying the not-inexpensive menu. This group doesn't always stop to complete surveys and is frequently missed by focus group recruiters. But there they are, right there in front of you. Museums for the past ten years have been attracting young people with borrowed interest campaigns of cheese, wine, and Friday nights. That's fine for building new audiences, but there's also a segment whose hearts you already own. When you see them at table after table, different stratagems for retention and membership start to take shape.

Look at the middle-aged couple, another ideal target. They were companionable and looked comfortable with their day, just the kind of visitor who probably will return for another pleasant experience. They probably support many arts interests: attending theater, buying concert series, dining out frequently, or volunteering time and money. They stand right in the crosshairs of your fund-raising targeting. They are your ambassadors, the people who bring friends and transmit word-of-mouth approbation. Relaxing over lunch, they have time to reflect on the museum's offerings.

READERS AND INFORMATION GATHERS

The two women didn't linger, but they remain an appetizing target because among the items they were toting were brochures and schedules. Other research might miss this important data. It likely would not reveal the literature that "fifty-year-old females from suburban ZIP codes" carry with them. Observational research delves beyond superficial descriptions to show that this market segment reads up on their visit and studies their brochures throughout the day. Perhaps if they had more to read, they would have stayed longer.

Clearly, they had a route planned through the museum and wanted to get on with it. So short lunches don't mean lack of interest. Whatever their ongoing intentions, these diners are also information eaters, an important insight that you can build on to develop Sunday sightseers into more committed members of your fold.

As for the eat-and-run people, their demographics would mislead you. They almost certainly were museum lovers, cognoscenti even, and every box they might check on a survey would suggest involvement and ongoing support for museums in general. However, they weren't involved in the museum they visited that day; they didn't sit together long enough to share and reflect and absorb its distinctive experience. They represent every marketer's nightmare: the customer who has actually purchased the product yet doesn't care enough to commit to it.

These missed opportunities are what museum marketers try to avoid by meeting and embracing appropriate customers, keeping them close, and never letting them forget the unique pleasures of the product. Ever see a chef come over to the table of regular customers? There are analogous ways to reward good customers in your institution.

Other museums, other days, yield other insights that don't appear in a focus group or survey.

At 11:30 A.M. at the Art Institute of Chicago, people start assembling for lunch, either at the white tablecloth restaurant or the cafeteria. By 12 noon there are lines, and by 12:30 there are crowds. Many museums have similarly successful lunch hours, but there are visitor insights that good cash register receipts—albeit excellent types of research—don't tell you. For example, on the day of observation, 85 percent of the tables, in both the cafeteria and the sit-down venue, were occupied by more than one person. It appears that folks who eat out, even in the nonintimidating confines of a museum, prefer company. On this specific observation, the company must have been very good because there was much talk and laughter and, except for a small minority, no flipping open of cell phones. In the entire room, over a period of forty-five minutes, only three people were speaking on mobile phones. Most of the diners were women, although that day one out of three visitors was men. At three of the thirty tables, diners had already made a purchase at the museum store. Although most of the people were adults, there were several adult-teenager and young-adult groups. A few diners, with ID lanyards, appeared to be museum staff. Everyone in the waiting area was part of a multiple or waiting for lunch companions. It was a social setting, a place for peer sharing and peer learning.

MARKET SEGMENTS AT THE LUNCH TABLE

Finally, here's a brief description of five other group segments, this batch observed at the Nelson-Atkins Museum of Art in Kansas City, Missouri, on a weekday:

Senior twosome reading brochures, eating quickly.

Man in business suit with old man in sweater, likely son–father lunch

Young adult in jeans and a hoodie with two forty-year-old women and a grandmother type

Two brisk, thirty-something women with businesslike folders

Middle-aged man and woman with camera equipment and walking boots

Some of these descriptions are totally subjective—guesswork—but they demonstrate how easily observation leads to imagining, which leads to a reinvestigation of your visitor market segments.

Behind this simple data collection, which any staffer at any museum could collect, waits a long agenda of possible subject to discuss with your staff: capitalizing on shoppers, encouraging solo visitors, giving the groups something to discuss, planning for men, attracting nontraditional museumgoers, and reevaluating the senior stereotype. You see visitors differently when they're at ease. By the way, this is a good time for your employees to observe them, the dining area being one of the few places where they intersect with the customer.

IMPLICATIONS: BEARINGS AND BONDING

If the food service managers were conducting this research, they'd undoubtedly want to further quantify it. To run a successful restaurant, numbers and broad demographics affect menu, pricing, staffing, size of tables, and hours of operation. For other managers and marketers within your museum, the behavior of the lunchtime crowd suggests many more refinements and spurs new thinking.

The dining area, including the waiting area, imitates the lobby in helping visitors get their bearings. It's a decompression room, transitioning visitors from their own world to your world. It's a debriefing area where they can summarize what they've seen. Here, first-time customers will see what kinds of people like museums and be reassured that it's people like them. They'll see moms with strollers, senior men accompanying their wives, children who are free to explore, and teenagers who actually seem happy. This is crucially important for reassuring the novice and implanting the idea of repeat visits. In research with college students, many said that the museums weren't for young people like them. When asked if they knew anyone who did visit museums, they realized that many of their friends did, in fact, enjoy museums very much. By "looking around," if only in their mind's eye, they revised their statement. Sitting down at a table gives visitors—and you—a vantage point for viewing.

One particular market segment stands out: visitors in multiples. We tend to think about individual members of a market segment, not three- or four-person groups. They form a distinct cohort, neither individuals nor couples, and deserve evaluation.

On one side, almost any marketing initiative improves if it's multiplied. If two or three people sit down, review the experience, and remind themselves how worthwhile the visit is, it's better than one person sitting down and considering it by himself. When two people see a table tent promoting the next exhibition, it's two prospective repeat visitors. When three people get up restored and ready to shop at the store, that's more revenue for the store. When a group of people talk over lunch, that's buzz, the beginning of powerful word-of-mouth advertising. One person may reflect and talk to others later, and that's a valuable recommendation, but the words come more easily when developed *en groupe*, and their validity grows, too.

Groups need a dining room because they need a place to gather. Singletons need a dining room because it's a safe place to be alone. In smaller markets or residential areas where dining alternatives don't exist, the museum restaurant as a haven could convince the singleton and become a major marketing tool for attracting and keeping this market segment.

The best scenario casts the museum as a matchmaker, engaging individual visitors so thoroughly that they want to return with companions. There are many opportunities for developing the restaurant to accomplish this feat. The menu itself, if distinctive enough, will position the museum as a lunch destination and encourage bringing friends. Appeals to the business community frequently result in group meals. Children's portions signal a commitment to family groups and could also be promoted to school groups. Affordable pricing will make it easier for anybody to join a group that goes out to lunch. At the other end of the scale, more expensive menus will put the restaurant firmly in the destination category, a chancier position, as any restaurant manger will affirm, but also a powerful lure for the ladies-who-lunch segment.

DRILL-DOWN BY SITTING DOWN

A lot of drill-down is not necessary. As a marketing consultant puts it, "It's time finally to . . . do ethnography to find out what's going on from the shopper perspective and use . . . a spirit of internal cooperation to do something about the [issues] it unveils." If you have a restaurant or small café, regular observations will reveal all the insights you can handle. All you have to do is eat there yourself and look around. You'll be amazed at how much you can learn from nonverbal behavior. However, some surprises beg further exploration. The young parents enjoying a nonparental respite represent one modern psychographic definitely worth studying further. And remember, you're not trying to research the menu, meal prices, or other dining questions. You're leveraging the dining room as a means to insights.

Focus groups delve deeper into notions that arise from your observations and can be recruited by putting notices on table tents, at the cash register, or at the information desk. You can conduct the groups in the dining room, but don't serve more than beverages. Food is costly and distracting and is never included except at after-work sessions where light, quick snacks are provided. Remember that focus groups are directional, not projectable. They focus on one segment, such as visitors in groups, or on one topic you want to explore. They substantiate hunches or expose a wider range of views, but they don't solve your problem. They zoom in on individual responses but strive only for clarity, not consensus. Sometimes someone will burst out with a comment that never would have occurred to you in a year of reading surveys. This is thrilling, but it also starts the research cycle all over again. Focus groups are qualitative, not quantitative; however, having outlined all the things a focus group can't do, here are some good questions to start the conversation that can do you good:

Do you eat lunch at museums—this one or others? Under what circumstances?

How long do you spend? How is this different from eating lunch elsewhere?

With whom do you eat? Is it different when you meet at the museum?

Describe a typical lunchtime experience. What do you talk about?

Describe a pleasant museum restaurant experience.

Would you ever just eat at a museum restaurant without visiting the exhibits?

Describe a typical lunch group.

Are museums good places for groups? Why?

Do you ever visit a museum alone? How is it different from visiting with a group?

If you have to justify this research to your board, remind the members that the restaurant is one place where people talk, compare impressions, and reinforce the positive experience of the visit. Maybe it's where they'll plan for their next visit or learn about the next exhibition. If it's a large museum or a destination museum, the dining table provides fuel for the next round of galleries or the store. Lunch as a pit stop gives visitors the energy to stop at the information desk for a membership brochure or simply to leave happy and not exhausted. As the nineteenth-century French gourmand Brillat-Savarin (1825) said, *la table* is a sort of ceremony where man can celebrate his intellectual power and fire up his energies.

10

Taking Photos

Turn the observing lens, for a moment, on the picture taker, that significant subspecies of museum visitor who is always framing, focusing on, and observing others. Some photographer categories dominate. First the family chronicler, who documents family vacations compulsively and minutely. You see him, usually a man, lining the kids up in front of the building, occasionally asking a passerby to get a shot of the whole family. Sometimes it's a young man snapping his girlfriend or a middle-aged man with lots of optical equipment hanging from his neck, helping his wife document their fabulous trip. Then there's the would-be artiste photographer, who shoots your façade from interesting angles. You are an important destination to this photographer, who wanders back and forth and around your architecturally important building, sometimes even going inside. The comedian photographer acts like an aspiring film director, carefully posing his family and friends into weird positions to shoot them interacting with your more unusual sculptures, artifacts, or scientific models. Another type whose quietness belies his or her potential is the photographer scholar, who, with the permission of museum policy, takes close-ups of the exhibit itself. This visitor is engrossed by the exhibits and spends a lot of time looking at them before shooting.

As museums marketers explore ways to better understand their audiences, both to attract new visitors and to retain current ones, look at the people who look through lenses because they are spending extra time and thought in and around your museum. Picture taking reveals so much about the photographers themselves that it pays to observe them individually. You'll see some compelling audience motivation. Not everyone snaps photos, of course, but enough do to expand your thinking about different market segments and different ways to reach your visitors.

FAMILY CHRONICLER

The family chronicler belongs to the largest photographer group and reflects the majority attitude, that museums are significant landmarks in one's personal and family life. This huge segment has always occupied and will continue to demand the bulk of your attention. This traditional visitor approaches your threshold with a time-honored purpose: to be enlightened or entertained and to feel good enough about his experience to flaunt it to others: "And here we are in front of the Blacksmith Shop." This mom or dad, student or honeymooner, tourist or frequent traveler, will invariably love your museum, remember it in surprising detail, and remain casually loyal because he has a memory and a proof he can show off for years. Among visitor types, he ambles in the lower reaches of involvement—he's an all-inclusive sightseer—but in the upper levels of satisfaction. He and his family will be word-of-mouth ambassadors and loyalists, the kind of customer every museum craves. You can nurture and harvest family photographers and enhance their and their families' involvement. For example, if you're the museum that sells camera memory cards, he'll remember you distinctively and maybe spend even more lens time with your institution. You can provide photo-op sections of the museum to boost scrapbooking efforts and use your digital terminals to help photographers turn snapshots into postcards. These camera-toting visitors, tourists or locals, are genetically coded to search for memories and experiences. They are a rich base for ongoing communication, brand building, and all that follows, from repeat visits to word-of-mouth to membership to higher levels of support.

ARTISTE PHOTOGRAPHER

With everyone toting professional-looking cameras, the small club of artiste photographers might escape notice. In fact, since everyone steps aside for cameramen composing shots, they're likely causing remark outside your building, even if they never get inside where you can see them. But these visual and deliberate photographers spend a lot of time looking very carefully; a visually appealing museum, above and beyond its objects, resonates strongly with this group. If yours is an architecturally distinctive museum, visitors with an artistic bent are an obvious audience to be nurtured and grown, one to be greeted with what amounts to professional courtesy. Maybe you offer them special admission to artist talks or an invitation to a future event that you return with the camera bag that's checked in the coatroom. Maybe you set aside a room or area for photography or design a brochure outlining your most photogenic, permissible displays. The no-photos-allowed policy makes sense generally, but not all visitors are general. Museums provide libraries for scholars, and it might make sense to provide an analogous space for serious photographers. At the very least, the staff on duty can apologize sincerely and admire the camera profusely while still shaking a warning finger at gallery shots. One way to cater to this special group: if your building or landscaping is noteworthy, set aside a day or night just for photographers; it's a good way to gather names of this market segment.

Realize that the absorbed artiste photographer may be more interested in his art than your exhibits. It's quite likely that he doesn't enjoy museums as much as he collects interesting compositions. However, even thought you may be just another interesting face, you can lure this photographer inside and direct his gaze to your content. Although this visitor is really just window-shopping, admiring what's pretty or nifty and not intending to get involved, he can be persuaded to look at you as distinctive. Emphasize your distinct personality and vision. Mount photo displays in the lobby to tell your story in a language photographers understand. Add a field in your database for photography buffs and send specialized mailings to them. Stage a Photo Day and offer opportunities to shoot, attend lectures, and network. Partner with photo stores. And be scrupulous with the photographic images in your own material; hire good photographers, designers, and printers to ensure lucid, well-articulated communications. Artiste photographers look at you in ways you probably don't look at yourself, so follow their gaze and be glad they're attracting so much attention.

COMEDIAN PHOTOGRAPHER

The comedian deserves more study than seems warranted at first blush. After all, this is the man or woman who takes up space and obscures others' sight lines while he composes his witty photos involving his friends and family and your precious objects. However, his complete absorption with the museum and its objects is a trait to be nurtured, as this photographer already feels at home and at ease; he is already a familiar. This person is more sensitive and thoughtful than you might think: he looks at a new object and really sees it, arranging his wife's limbs to mimic the oil portrait on the wall, placing his son just so next to the model of the brain. And, of course, he's making a memory that is specific and meaningful, not a generic group shot on the front steps but a composition that integrates your collection with his family. Unlike the chronicler, who acts automatically, the comedian thinks, plans, and makes connections. If photo compositions were donations, his would be at a higher level.

The implications are exhilarating. This interactive visitor wants to touch you and be a part of the museum, and you need to abet this involvement without endangering everything in the gallery. It takes the same skill as any interactive exhibit and is a challenge for curators and educators. Some museums make or designate touchable objects, and you probably have many photo props available already in the architectural details of your building, landscaping features, and furnishings. It's worth thinking about because comedian photographers, like street performers, draw the attention of others. With their incisive photo setups, they're like docents without a portfolio, pointing out interesting aspects of your objects that other visitors might not notice.

People-plus-props is not just for witty visitors: the charm of people interacting with the artifacts specific to your museum adds impact to your advertising and public relations photography. Your major donors would enjoy having their photos taken with an object their contribution supports, and no photo of your board should be without one.

SCHOLAR PHOTOGRAPHER

Scholars who take photographs to document or substantiate their studies make up an elite group: they are very knowledgeable about your exhibits, and they have successfully received your permission to shoot. They already connect strongly with your institution and appreciate your scholarship, and you should make every effort to maintain your relationship. Scholars may become frequent visitors, members, and supporters, and they undoubtedly move in circles that also appreciate your focus. Like any other visitor, scholars have friends and children, and when you facilitate them professionally, you entice them personally. If you can't permit photos, perhaps you can help them in other research endeavors. You can always give them free passes for their colleagues or family. Narrow market segments, like serious photographers, inspire broader thinking about the ways you can nurture all your visitors.

OBSERVE THE CAMERA EQUIPMENT

You can also broaden your ways of perceiving visitor motivation. You don't have to stare at the people; just look at their gear. The range and complexity of visiting photographers' equipment, from simple mobile phones to expensive lenses and meters, signal a few personality traits. Let's start with the latest equipment and their owners: young people with cameras in their phones. They are in constant and devoted communication—visual and aural—with their peers. Their shots will appear on social networking sites everywhere and forever. They take pictures all the time of all their minutest activities. They have a need to be in touch, to connect, to have many friends, and to be understood and remembered. Museums already accommodate the need for social interaction and, considering the motivations of young photo takers and uploaders, may want to make new accommodations for the mobile age. For a start, try a blog for visual contributors or a Web link for visitors' Facebook pages. And don't make young people stop at the lobby. Set a camera-equipped laptop on a counter at the museum store checkout and let the one-handed photography crowd take pictures with your merchandise as props.

Bulkier equipment hangs from the shoulders of retired men, a growing visitor segment that carries bigger and more serious cameras. In a culture where men retire earlier and live more vigorously, where second careers and avocations flourish, high-level photography is very popular. It would seem that wives, who used to have trouble getting men to travel, now need only throw out the bait of a good photo-op, and the trip is on. Museums are always popular travel destinations and can capitalize on this new category of tourist/travelers.

Some photography behavior is undoubtedly local or dictated by individual museum policy. On the day I visited the Shanghai Museum, the majority of visitors were armed with professional-looking cameras, carefully studying the encased artifact before squeezing off a shot. They were solemnly on a mission rather than casually strolling and viewing. Whether this is widespread behavior or a fluke that day is irrelevant. As with any observational research, unexpected behavior is to be welcomed as a mind opener, and before you wonder about its universality, wonder about what it might mean in your universe. As with kids on their phones or men on a new hobby, the thought of visitors on a personal research project is beguiling. Can you appeal to the amateur researcher as a market segment? Can you attract family chroniclers, artistes, and comedians? The implications are intriguing.

IMPLICATIONS

People who take photographs are visual, and their style of learning might be visual as well. As discussed in another chapter, there are four learning styles—visual, aural, read and kinetic—and a museum, like a classroom, should prepare to interpret for all of them.

The lure of photography has revolutionized communications, via YouTube and social networking sites like Facebook. Realize that when you see a photographer in your museum, you have a potential reporter in your midst—for good or for mischief.

Photography is an integral part of many people's day, and it can play a bigger, more distinguished part in your museum. Look around—everywhere from the lobby to the back hallways—and see if you could use photography more elegantly. Check the bulletin boards for the amount of photographic images relative to written or computer-illustrated communications. Look at your website, both the static and the interactive pages, and evaluate the quality of the photography. And review your newsletter, whether printed or online, for its photojournalism. Photography has been with us for 150 years, and we take it for granted. Yet many people are seeing it with a newly discriminating eye, and that helps you with any photo-enhanced story.

Of course, it's digital technology that abets photography, and with it come dangers. More people setting off flashes near your objects is always a problem. Intellectual property infringement is a new and growing challenge. Security, liability, and misinformation are lurking dangers. On the upside, the Internet also helps you find solace as well as solutions for your problems. Considering all the issues brought to the forefront by technology, you might want to investigate this photography phenomenon more fully, to drill down into the motivations of the photographers.

DRILL-DOWN

Since most photographs end up on the Internet or in e-mail, an online survey is the logical way to probe the photographers. A survey on your website, perhaps in conjunction with a photo promotion, might include the following questions:

What do you look for when taking a photo at our—or any—museum?

How much of your visit do you spend in taking pictures?

Who sees the photos besides you?

Thinking of photos that friends have sent to you or displayed elsewhere, which were the most interesting?

Do you enter photo competitions? If so, do you compete for the prize or the recognition or to show friends?

Looking at these age-groups, tell briefly what kinds of shots you took at different ages. Answer as many as you want:

10–14

15–19

20–30

30–40

50–60

60–75

What one photo on our website interests you most?

This questionnaire is designed for dialog boxes to encourage verbatim responses. If you want, you can limit the size of the box and the number of words.

Since young people enjoy photography so much and use it so easily, try using it as both a research and a teaching tool. It's is a win-win. Enlist field trip classes to bring cameras—or you supply them—and have each child photograph the part of the museum he or she enjoys the most. Tell them that they can shoot anything, anywhere, from the time they walk in your door until they pick up their coats and backpacks. They can take pictures of the front door, any exhibit, any small detail of an exhibit, a wall panel, a piece of furniture, or a sign. They can take a picture of a friend or the teacher, but there must be some part of the museum in the picture. Give them a CD or a flash drive to save their images and offer the services of an information systems staffer to help the teacher upload the shots. Ask if they'd be willing to add notes or commentary to their slide show. The students will have a more meaningful and memorable museum tour, and you'll have a visual report of the small details adult eyes often miss.

Continue watching photographers, and you will undoubtedly spot other variations of the type. They are worth looking for because photographers care enough to get involved with your institution, to stop and look at it from different angles, to immerse themselves in it, and to have a good time with it. They see themselves as part of the picture, which is exactly what you want from your visitors.

It would be wrong to dismiss any of these photo takers as mere tourists, here today and gone home tomorrow. In the contracting global world, where travel is common and memories are made to be e-mailed, a museum visit spreads and grows. The people behind and in the viewfinder will return, tell their friends, visit a partner institution, follow your exhibitions and projects online, and purchase from your store whenever they want. Look at picture takers as a very demonstrative form of museum lover and think how you can leverage their affection.

11

Early Birds

As the two workmen carried the Australian flag to the flagpole outside Melbourne's National Gallery of Victoria, International, one lone woman was already standing and waiting. Soon another appeared, sat on the reflecting pool balustrade, and watched the flag being raised. It would be fifteen more minutes before the museum doors opened—moments of calm zeal but not much else.

The world is divided into two kinds of people: those who get there early and everybody else. First arrivers afflict all institutions: undergrads who are in their seats before the teacher reaches the parking lot, voters who cause polling places to open before dawn, and baseball fans lined up in sleeping bags to buy the first ticket. Sometimes duty drives these customers, sometimes schedules, and sometimes pure unadulterated loyalty.

At the front door of many museums, early bird behavior can be observed, and the reasons reveal opportunities if not problems. In any town, on any day, one can see block-long lines waiting to enter a blockbuster exhibition, public transportation users whose schedules put them at the door thirty minutes early, and school buses and tour buses that always arrive slightly before the stated hour. In each case, the anticipation is heightened by the wait, but there's another way to look at this. Maybe the promise is delayed and diluted. Perhaps those customers who just can't wait to get inside your museum chafe at the wait. It deserves further research.

There are cultural changes afoot that make early arrivals more a trend than a curiosity. As everyone's life speeds up and time contracts, traditional hours may start to look dated. Working hours have become more flexible, discretionary, and fluid. School schedules are modifying, with not only students but also their parents, teachers, and bus drivers having to adapt. Older people get up earlier and prefer daytime activities. And many businesses and organizations that used to hold lunch meetings now find breakfast a less costly meal.

Consider the realities of today's travel business. Hotel rooms are available later in the day, and they kick you out earlier. Travelers cram more of their sightseeing into fewer days and longer hours. Tourists on a budget will drive longer hours to get to their destination; maybe they'll arrive late and want to leave early in the morning; perhaps they'll make more stops along the way. It's possible that other tourist and convention attractions will start to adjust their hours, and it might be worthwhile to check around with your local colleagues and competitors. The cost of opening a museum earlier is not to be trivialized, but some further research might suggest some bridges between early arrivers and the moment the doors actually open.

DRILL-DOWN

If you find even eight people waiting for your doors to open, send a staffer out with a short questionnaire to keep them engaged and, importantly at this stage of the discovering process, give you some deeper understanding into their motivations. Start the questionnaire with "Thank you for visiting us today" and then ask questions, adaptable to your own museum, like these:

How far did you travel to get here today? _____

How long have you been waiting? _____

Have you visited us before? _____

How long a wait is acceptable? _____

In order to help us make everyone's experience more enjoyable, please tell us what, if any, factors affected your early arrival (for example, website information, hotel, transportation, family schedule) _____

Which of the following would make the wait more pleasant?:

- Literature about the museum
- Information about the exhibition
- Museum staffer to answer questions
- Coffee or snack cart
- Merchandise cart
- Place to sit
- Entertainment on the plaza

Early birds' squeaks—not squawks, yet—have been receiving attention from other arts organizations. Theaters now have earlier curtains, and some are experimenting with morning, lunchtime and "rush-hour" performances. This represents quite a culture shift, and the trend might be more tsunamic than previously supposed.

12

Shopping for Memories

As the two women left the museum store, they were laughing and practically dancing, their shopping bags bobbing in their hands. Two feet outside, they stopped, dove into the bags, and brought out their treasures to show each other. Of all the animated couples leaving a museum (and this animated behavior has been noted in other chapters), shoppers are the most manic of all. That people love to shop—and Americans may be just the most glaring example—is no secret, and the psychology of purchasing and owning is minutely studied. However, observational research in a museum helps one realize the depth of feeling in shopping, its ineffable power to please the museum visitor. *Souvenir* is more than the French word for "remembrance"; it is a magic token that conjures up many layers of enduring feelings, and museum shopping taps into the emotions of supporting a greatly enjoyed institution.

One of the reasons memories are so important to museum marketing is that memories beget action. Memories remind both the buyer and the recipient of museum merchandise of a rewarding time spent at your institution and, in many cases, actually prod them into revisiting that experience. Visitors will return not only to see the exhibits but also to buy gifts and personal items. People who have never visited will receive a museum store gift and consider a first visit. More powerfully than a direct-mail piece or bring-a-friend coupon, souvenirs from the store reach out across time and distance, communicating not merely an interesting education or social opportunity but also a belonging to a worthwhile organization. Memories help instill loyalty, the kind of loyalty that ramps up a visit into a lifelong involvement.

Psychological and even neurological studies emphasize the physical hold that an acquisition has over the acquirer. Neuroeconomist Gregory Berns refers to the "endowment effect" in describing the human internal wiring that conditions us to hold on to what we already have, to treasure it very highly. Purchases are a capitalistic expression of fascination, says Bruce Newman, a marketing professor at DePaul University in Chicago, speaking of the way Americans gobbled up Barack Obama presidential merchandise. Shopping is how Americans show emotion. An exploratory version of this concept has been shown in my own focus group research in which participants described in detail their deep attachment to museum purchases, some bought twenty years earlier.

Shoppers also contribute to the bottom line. Across the spectrum of museums, earned income—including revenue from stores—contributes 43.7 percent of U.S. museums' support.

TALK, COMPARE, CONSULT, REFLECT

But that is down the road. For the immediate future, consider your happy visitor who, for ten minutes to an hour, inspects, touches, discusses, ponders, and buys, all the while equating the shopping experience with everything else your museum has to offer. Look more closely at your own store and then at the behavior of the shoppers.

Your memory maker, for that is what a museum store is, has many means at its command. There are aisles where one can walk back and forth without having to follow a logical pattern as one does in the galleries. There are sales assistants to talk out loud with, a freedom not often exercised in the exhibit areas. And not only will museum staff help visitors relive the visit, but they'll do it knowledgeably as well. Whether volunteer or salaried, merchandisers are the type of people who know how to tell and sell. They are trained to know the merchandise and, by extension, the objects they reflect. To this point, the store can even expand on the learning in the galleries, with informative labels identifying the objects and relating them to exhibits. Currently, for-profit retailers are paying new interest to "homemade" signs—the daily specials and remarks handwritten on chalkboards at coffee shops and supermarkets; this idea can be easily adapted to your retail operation. Obviously, the selection of items reflects the tone and personality of your museum, and so, too, does the manner and quantity in which they are displayed.

Location, location, location applies to store real estate, just as it does to business and residential. Stores are usually located in the lobby, and this entrance—which is also the exit—is a crucial juncture where visitors get their introduction to a new experience and their summation of it. The store is well positioned to support the first impression and the lasting impression.

Other arts organizations realize the importance of tangible memory, and theater companies large and small have lobby kiosks or bookstalls stocked with appropriate merchandise. As at museums, they are wings of the education department.

WHAT SHOPPERS LOOK DOWN ON

I've discussed in another chapter the pattern of shoppers turning right. There's a corollary instinct to turn down: to incline the head and eyes downward at items on the shelf. Shoppers come in all heights, and they're interested in all kinds of merchandise, but when it comes to reaching, touching, or reading, they like to gaze down. This observation was made at the San Francisco Museum of Modern Art one morning in December, shortly before Christmas, when there was a lot of traffic, a good sample from which to make conjectures. If these shoppers were drawn by a caricaturist, they would be identified by the sharp angle of heads on neck: pointed decidedly down. Even tall people look to the lower shelves and peruse items on table displays rather than those on higher shelves. People who look up or at eye level don't touch or take an item to study. The few who do glance at items on high shelves look much longer at the ones on lower shelves. A very tall man who spent an hour killing time while his wife shopped her heart out hardly ever raised his head to the many books and decorative items on the higher shelves, even though surely he was challenged to find new material to ease his boredom. One woman examined a small box that held a set of napkin rings. This item was displayed on two shelves, one at shoulder height and one at the level of her wrist. She opted to pick up and read the box on the lower shelf. Even at the toy racks, where attractive and novel toys hung on higher pegs, grandparents and parents looked straight ahead. These indulgent folks probably would have considered items at any price point—but apparently not at any height point.

BOOKSHELF AND COMPUTER SCREEN HEIGHT

Other arts and learning institutions reveal the downward-looking tendency of human beings. In movie theaters, no one sits in the front rows; they'd have to look up. Library bookshelves reach no more than six feet high. Supertitles at the opera are being reexamined because they force the eyes up too high, and currently seat-back subtitles are gaining proponents.

The angle of eyesight has been defined carefully by ergonomics experts studying computer screens. The federal agency charged with overseeing worker safety and health, the Occupational Safety and Health Administration, stipulates that the most comfortable computer position is with the top of the monitor at or below eye level so that the center of the screen is fifteen to twenty degrees below eye level—in other words, looking down.

There are good reasons for museum visitors to work at lower levels as well. It is easier to look down at the full covers of books on the display tables and then pick them up to read further; even browsers at the bookshelves, after reading the spines, pulled books from the lower shelves and read heads down. It is easier to rearrange items after you've pulled them from the shelf. A very tall woman was seen looking at note cards on a lower shelf and then patting them back into neat piles. But she didn't tidy up the higher shelves. Even at her height, it was easier to work looking down.

IMPLICATIONS: TOYS AND GRANDPARENTS

Today, museum stores usually hire professionally trained, if not professional, merchandisers, and when it comes to displaying merchandise, there are sound rationales for shelf placement. The children's toys seem to offer a lesson in profitability because the cheap, shrink-wrapped gizmos are hung on peg boards below eye level, and the expensive, unique toys are on shelves higher up. If these mass-produced items are more profitable, they are placed wisely. However, if the unique toys could lend cachet and more profits to the museum, they are misplaced on high shelves and should be lower down.

And there are other marketing considerations that make the museum marketer think twice about the angle of the jaw of its customers. Staying in the toy section for a moment, consider the market segments who shop there. The most important are doting grandparents who, like many people over fifty years of age visiting a museum, might likely be travelers with discretionary money to spend. Good merchandisers will make it easy for them to spend on their special visit. But there's another group of grandparents in your store: local, retired, and educated. In addition to above-average disposable income, they might also have above-average interest in becoming a member or donor and a circle of acquaintances who could become buzz, or word-of-mouth, visitors. Stores should target these customers with a wide range of gift-appropriate merchandise and, when the sales are made, capture additional data about the purchasers. If your grandparent-age shoppers are the types to linger in a store for more than the average seven minutes (the observed time in larger stores only; the time might be different depending on the size of individual stores), they may be browsers, not buyers, but still an important psychographic segment. These are visitors who enjoy being everywhere in the museum, absorbing everything you have to offer. Make it easy for them to look, touch, and read looking down; they are also gathering memories. More data about their preferences should also be collected.

PARENTS WITH SECOND LIVES

The second significant segment is parents accompanying children, the solid demographic aged twenty-five to fifty-four that all marketers want and that museums should nurture. This robust demographic will become members and, with diligence, donors and supporters of your institution. Beyond your building, they lead lives of great importance to you: in the social, business, education, and civic community. They help form the opinions that ease the way for cultural institutions to succeed and prosper. For adults with children, items at the preferred below-eye level can be examined comfortably and selected quickly. For all adults, those expensive, one-of-a-kind items on the higher shelves would do better at eye level, where they can be not only seen but also admired at leisure, evaluated, and even touched. These items are brand builders, distinctive to the individual museum and capable of enhancing the museum's image long after purchase. They may be difficult to store and possibly less profitable, but they reinforce a museum's identity with the audience most immediately likely to become donors and even patrons.

The purchase cycle starts with looking but doesn't end at checkout, and that's where shopping bags come in. These will appear for some time on the street and as lunch bags, and many potential visitors will see them. You can't underestimate the number of eyes who will see your museum because they have seen your shopping bag; it is a marketing tool by itself and gains even more significance on the arm of a person whom others respect. Survey respondents have said that they feel more cultured and more discriminating carrying such a distinctive token. They are confident giving a gift from a museum; they like the association it conveys.

The third important market segment is children, who will be accruing enduring experiences from the minute they step inside your doors and who can motivate purchases that will become memories for life. For small children, it makes sense to display inexpensive, impulse purchases at the lowest levels. An important segment, of course, includes people in wheelchairs. In another chapter, you'll discover that the mobility impaired are a more significant part of your audience that you might suppose, but for now consider accessibility not only for their hands but also for their eyes.

When you see the prevalence of downcast eyes, you wonder about other aspects of your operation. As curators review the height of exhibits, labels, and video monitors, they might study their visitors in the store. It might make sense to lower bulletin boards, brochure racks, and interactive screens. (Tall guards who visitors have to look up to? Maybe you can provide them with chairs so that they, too, appear at eye level.)

DRILL-DOWN

Museum stores need to learn more about their customers, and the capabilities of the register are available to you as they are to any retailer. As you compile sales figures, you are also collecting item names, time of day, season of year, and member number. Find out from your suppliers what other information you can collect at the register. A variant of the register and a digital version of the comment card is a laptop at the counter where shoppers can enter information while waiting for a purchase to be paid or wrapped. The low-tech equivalent is a comment card, which, if worded thoughtfully, can gather useful additional information while offering significant customer incentives.

The following questionnaire prompts useful responses regardless of whether you use a laptop or a written comment card. The questions are designed for all types of museums—history, science, historic home, heritage, art museum, living history, and special interest—and, more important, for a variety of consumers. Some questions are geared to people who might become members, donors, volunteers, patrons, sponsors, or trustees. Some questions will engage the companions of shoppers, those who only stand and wait.

Thank you for visiting our museum. Your comments will help us keep the shelves and tables stocked with the kind of books and merchandise you like. Please include your name, address and e-mail for discounts when you return.

Name three holidays or events, such as Mothers Day, New Home, or Graduation, when you buy gifts that you might select at our store:

What items:

Interested you most when you first walked in?
Surprised you most?
Would you select for a child age five to ten?
Appeal to a teenager?
Stimulate your interest in a topic that we might explore in a special program or lecture?
Best typify our community? State? Region? Neighbors?
Give insights into our history? New ideas in science? The world of art?
Represent the mission of personality of the museum that you would recommend to an acquaintance who wanted to know more about us?
Would you return to purchase, even if you weren't visiting the rest of the museum?

Think of one friend with a birthday in the next month. What item currently available comes closest to what you would select for him or her?

Please list birthdays of family members. Discounts will be available for one month prior to the day.

Importantly, these are leading questions that stimulate internal discussion among the museum staff regardless of how or even whether they are answered. In these discussions, your store personnel will provide surprisingly poignant insights. After all, they are in a good position to closely observe customers and interact with them at some length. The behavior noted in the stores will provide ripple-out ideas for implementation throughout the museum.

13

Handheld Children: The New Demographic

A grandmother, to distract her five-year-old grandson, told him to look around the gallery and find something he particularly liked. He quickly pulled her over to a minor figure, occupying an obscure corner of a huge historic painting. Why was he attracted by this sketchily rendered, fallen peasant and not the hero in gleaming armor on a rearing horse? Because the figure on the lower periphery was all the thirty-inch-high person could see. Preschoolers are condemned to walk forever attached to the hands of their elders, seeing precious little besides knees. These youngsters present an appealing target. Quite different from the older child on a school field trip, he or she appears only as an appendage to his parents; although he won't be a student-customer for a few years, he's a good prospect now.

Children age five to nine are surprisingly communicative if you use observational research to decipher what's on their minds and in their line of vision. Picture that almost cliché snapshot, photogenic and distinct, where the adult kneels down to child level and considers the exhibit with her child from the thirty-inch vantage point. Physically close together and absorbed, mother and child point at the work, talk to each other, and touch in a perfect harmony of hands-on teaching. This action repeats in museum after museum, and the only jarring part of the scene is how few of the exhibits hang low enough for the child to see.

For example, an observational walk-through of a particularly colorful exhibition at the MOCA Geffen, a satellite to the Museum of Contemporary Art in Los Angeles, counted only twenty-seven of sixty wall-mounted works whose bottom edge could be seen by thirty-inch-tall people. Yet this exhibition drew dozens of parents wanting to show this amusing, fun art to their small children. A similar tale unfolded at the Milwaukee Art Museum, where on a Sunday afternoon many parents and grandparents were strolling the galleries with children in hand. Yet in this large and impressive collection of modern art, very few pieces came to within thirty inches of the floor. In fact, even children of the forty-four-inch cohort, old enough to explore on their own, could see eye to eye with only a small percentage of the works. One girl, asked to point out one work in a small gallery that she liked, turned without thinking to the one that was her height. But on consideration, she pointed across the room to her real favorite, which she could see only from a distance. She had no way of studying the painting closely without craning her head back. In addition, there wasn't a label in the museum (or any museum) that she or her peers could stretch close enough to read.

To demonstrate the delight enjoyed by children who can actually see the piece, picture the five-year-old, seen by the author, squirming with delight under a Dale Chihuly glass sculpture. Children orient themselves to your exhibits in ways different than adults would even consider. It's chancy putting child and art in close proximity but kind of thrilling to see it from their sight lines.

UP TO YOUR ELBOW IN CHILDREN

To inventory the child's-eye number of items on display at any museum, art or otherwise, just walk around and see which exhibits reach down as far as your elbow (the part of an average adult that's thirty to thirty-six inches high, or the height of a five- to nine-year-old). The pickings are slim for youngsters without a ladder.

The same scarcity of child's-eye-level objects prevails at the museum store, an economic godsend or disaster, depending on whether one is the store manager or the parent. Most store furnishings whose height is less than forty inches from the floor are storage cabinets or stashes for larger objects. High above reach are the glitter and intrigue of toys and books selected to challenge young minds. There are several missed opportunities here. Children without anything to look at miss the educational factor on which museum stores are based. And when they whine and tug, they drag parents away from browsing and buying for themselves. Compare this with for-profit retail stores that address the restless companion with chairs, small chairs and tables, television monitors, and play areas. Museum stores don't need distractions for children, only to lower their racks.

LUNCHTIME

Another child-intensive area is the café, and here children of all ages play a role in the success of the institution. The café—or cafeteria, restaurant, or dining room—is the one place where every visitor is comfortable talking out loud. It's a place to sit down, admit fatigue, fuel up, and generally feel great about the museum experience. Tactically, the café is essential to the continuation of the visit if children are present. Children need, above all, their creature comforts: rest, food, and a bathroom. If the creature isn't happy, no one else will be. Strategically, the café encourages reflection, bonding, the interchange of ideas, and all the emotional and intellectual stimulation that builds and maintains the museum's place in the hearts and minds of families—the adults and the young visitors-to-be. Here again, there are few modifications for the thirty-inch person, and that's nearsighted because children contribute to the loyalty building that grows in the comfort of the lunch interlude. Children ask questions about what they see. Children force their parents to explain what the day is all about. Children want stuff from the store. For museums that are destinations and that occupy a greater chunk of the family's leisure day, food will become even more important. From a competitive perspective, the café might be the tiebreaker between one museum and another form of family tourist or leisure activity. Not only should child seating be provided, but so should images from the rest of the museum for small people to enjoy. As observed in another chapter, families with young children often stay in the café longer than any other group. They relax and talk longer than couples, women, groups or single diners. These uncomplaining children, these wheels that don't squeak, shouldn't be ignored. Many for-profit restaurants provide crayons and games for bored children; museum restaurants should also create materials to engage youngsters. If there were a way to sell items from the store at a location near the restaurant, think of the synergy that would exist between the forty-five minutes of lunchtime calm and museum-related objects to play and learn with. Visual delights are what keep the little guys engaged and give them the full experience that is their due.

HUNKER DOWN

Not too many people have the physical or mental flexibility to scrunch down to a child's level of seeing things, but one smart marketer did. At one rather lengthy meeting, Proctor & Gamble's Pampers brand ordered its managers and ad agencies to hit the floor and view the world from knee level. It was a great conversation starter, and you can imagine what would unfold if you did the same at your museum. Hunker down, consider the little thirty-inch-high person, and scan your domain. Look at the exhibits, labels, panels, benches and chairs, guards, brochure rack, distance to the bathroom, signage, reading level of the audio tour script, and training of adult tour docents. This is the museum that is seen by children tethered to the hands of adults; it is not the museum of family days. It is not a visit focused on the child, but it's frequently a first and formative visit, and you can make it unforgettably exciting.

Thinking from this angle has many benefits. First and foremost, since these youngsters are not the school field trip cohort that comprises your traditional way of serving children, you need to understand this new segment of young visitors. This group engages in the museum in a totally different way from the traditional family activities, which are directed only at kids. These families didn't come to the museum for kids' stuff at all; they're simply bringing the kids along.

TEACHERS AND DONORS

Looking to the future, demographers say, plan for fewer high school–age people, which means that the fourth-grade segment will also shrink. The already curtailed school field trip will continue to diminish as the numbers decrease. So, treat these five- to nine-year-olds as you do their fourth-grade siblings because as a group they are growing in importance. Looked at from another demographic perspective, today's five- to nine-year-olds will be adults in only fifteen years, when the impressions you sow now will start to bear fruit.

Add home schooling to the formula, and you have another new scenario for the broad category of family. Home-schooled children come to the museum with parents who are, in fact, their teachers. It's yet another market segment.

Parents of young children are, in the twenty-first century, likely to be older and more financially stable, so they are philanthropy targets, too. You might have them on your donor list because of their age or tenure as members, but as parents they represent a different psychographic from the traditionally older donor.

Parents of handheld children might also be foreign visitors, not the locals and tourists you typically think of. This brave new world deserves a lot of study, and as your museum mines the opportunities of the global tourist, include *les petits* in your vista.

Another way to look at the parents of a handheld child is from the psychographic perspective. Parents of singleton children—moms and dads of a resourceful youngster who quietly pads alongside—represent a psychographic segment that might be called the "parent couple." The parents I observed were absorbed in each other. While they attended to the self-sufficient child, they positively glowed with each other, enjoying their time in the museum as if it were an island vacation, separate, a little exotic, and stress free. Here two married adults can simply sit, talk quietly, and enjoy each other's company. Frequently, both parents of a single child are working, busy couples whose lives give them scant time to be together, and the museum becomes an institutional nanny. So now, in addition to first Fridays, singles nights, and young collectors' clubs, perhaps museums can add married-couples afternoons.

STROLLER CAREGIVERS

A variation of the dependent child, handheld variety, is the dependent child in a stroller. Here your focus is definitely the person pushing the stroller, and she's a more complex definition of that superficial demographic: the married mother age twenty-five to thirty-four. These women are visiting purely for themselves, and your museum can make the journey easier. You can also develop this consumer into a loyal customer by relating to her unique requirements. One thing she needs is socialization, a place to be with other women her own age. Then she needs mental stimulation. One piece of research from Sydney, Australia, accidentally turned up some fresh insights. The Museum of Natural History conducted a survey on electronic newsletters versus printed-and-mailed newsletters. The results, though small, revealed a habit, almost a ritual, that no one predicted. Young mothers loved the print version because they can put a printed publication in the back flap of the stroller and save it for a quiet moment. Moms pushing babies carry reading material with them and cherish museums for the quiet time they provide. Back in the Northern Hemisphere, look around and notice that women with strollers meet their peers with a gleesomeness that borders on fervor. When you think of these women as people who love to read, who need time to themselves, and who welcome the company of other women, you discover new ways to develop their involvement with the museum. By the way, not all members of these groups are mothers; some are nannies. By a fascinating twist of lifestyle, this target audience now consists of stay-at-home moms; women who work outside the home; women from widely separated ZIP codes, income levels, and ages; and women who often are from different ethnic groups.

How to cater to this mixed group? In terms of your facility, consider first its convenience for that bulky entity: caregiver-stroller-baby-accessory bag-stuff. Can it or they get up the steps, through the coatroom, into the restrooms, and around the galleries? If they're going to a toddler program, is there something down that corridor for the adult to pick up and read? Are there places for groups of moms to get together? Do you have promotional material to intrigue the adult into returning for another visit? Remember that today's baby carer will, in just a few years, be at liberty again to rejoin the museum as a member, donor, volunteer, or word-of-mouth ambassador.

But wait—rejoin? The mom/caregiver may never have been to a museum in her life before she started caring for children. As we see, the adult at the other end of a baby stroller is a complex market segment, one that a museum can address in many ways. In focusing on this segment, you will fine-tune everything from facilities to programming to promotional materials.

DRILL-DOWN: PARENTS, NOT FAMILIES

Now that you've seen the prevalence of small, handheld children in your museum, you might want to explore further their and their parents' attitudes. Little children are notoriously difficult to interview, so let's start off easy with a focus group of parents, screening for parents of five- to nine-year-olds who have taken their child along at least once on a visit that wasn't specifically child oriented. After age nine, children start going on school field trips, and their attitudes will be influenced by those trips. Also by age nine, many children acquire siblings, and the kind of visit discussed in this chapter becomes a more conventional family day. Recruit for parents of only children because there's a better chance of getting the *parent* perspective rather than the *family* perspective. There's a big difference.

Follow the focus group pattern of 1) introductions, 2) general questions about museum usage, 3) more specific questions about visits with their child, and 4) discussion-prompting questions. Use these questions as a guide:

When you and your spouse decide to visit a museum, is your child part of the decision?

When selecting a leisure activity for yourselves on the weekend, how often is your child the main consideration?

From what leisure activities—other arts events, sports events, working out, shopping, or dining—would you exclude your child?

How are museums different?

Did you visit museums together before you had a child?

Think about museum exhibitions you have enjoyed. Whether your child was with you or not, what part of that exhibition did or would your child enjoy?

Suppose that, in the past month, you visited a museum with your child. Describe your ideal weekend or leisure activity that you'd select for next month?

How often is your child the reason for a museum trip?

How often do you simply bring your child along?

What museums are favorites of yours?

When you travel, do you visit museums with your child?

At what point will you consider so-called family days or family programs at museums?

How will you help your child remember or interpret his or her school field trips?

How are your personal field trips different from the school trips?

Focus group questions sometimes seem repetitive, but different respondents respond to different kinds of questions. You have to probe, then probe some more. All these questions are designed to get two batches of information: what the child gets out of a visit at the end of his or her parents' hands and what the hand-holding parents experience.

However deeply you choose to explore these new market segments, plan a staff discussion session around them. Think about how your institution looks at children and parents, how it markets family days, and how it depicts families in promotional material. Then ask yourself how closely it applies to the two-parent/one-child scenario.

14

Long Lines and Smiles

On one cold, blustery, sleeting day in Chicago, the line for the Jasper Johns exhibition at the Art Institute stretched for half a block and twenty minutes. Once visitors got inside, there was another loop past the coatroom. Yet every single person greeted the ultimate checkpoint, the ticket taker, with a smile and often a hello. Actually, one out of the 100 didn't smile, but she was just frozen cold. This is not an isolated Midwest experience. In temperate Sydney, Australia, according to the marketing director of the Natural History Museum, nobody minds lines; a length-of-wait sign is all that is needed to keep the waiters happy.

The long-line observation is significant because it's so counterintuitive and because those smiles and hellos are so utterly sincere. When it comes to lining up for a popular exhibition, museumgoers stand with preternatural patience. Research from the *Journal of Hospitality and Leisure Marketing* (Geissler, Conway, Rucks, and Edison 2006) has shown that consumers believe that a good exhibition is "worth the wait," but you have to see the looks on their faces to know whether they are simply tolerating the wait or enjoying the anticipation. The smiles on the faces of the Art Institute visitors expressed tolerance and also enjoyment; they were already enthusiastic.

Focus groups would never reveal this enthusiasm because they take place after the fact. They provide the inestimable advantage of watching reactions to recollections and interactions between participants, but the viewer is observing facial expressions out of context, often months after the event. And the participants are sitting down in a cozy room; it isn't possible to see how they would really react to standing out in the elements. Participants might say "worth it" in a focus group to demonstrate how pro-museum they are; after all, they were recruited for the group on the basis of having visited a museum. But a thoughtful consideration of whether a wait was worth the trouble doesn't deliver half the punch of seeing those cheerful smiles.

The verity of visitors' statements on surveys also begs skepticism. They might say that a long line is "worth it" because that's the rational response, and people who take the time to complete a survey are logical types. But these are verbal questions and invoke verbal responses. You have to see the look on their faces, in situ, to evaluate visitors' emotional reaction.

Not all cultures stand in line the same way. Some cultural groups cluster and crowd peaceably toward the transaction. Britons require a queue. Americans seem happy with multiple lines and enjoy the game of trying to find the shortest one. In addition, lining up for an event promises a much better result than lining up for the checkout counter. So behavior in lines is complex, and there quite likely are opportunities as well as problems here. After all, lines are here to stay; we might as well cope with them.

IMPLICATIONS

Lines may be better understood if redefined as clusterings. There's excitement in crowds and camaraderie in groups of people, and to articulate these waits as pre-viewing experiences changes how the total visitor experience is assessed.

Think of lines and queues not simply as an aspect of crowd control but as extensions of the exhibition, the way the museum store extends learning and enjoyment. Busy restaurants offer complimentary appetizers to waiting diners, and museums could offer teasers of information in the form of fliers, maps, or laminated gallery guides. You could also borrow a page from airports where airline personnel work the queues to answer questions. You probably already enlist environmental design to plot a system of directional signs to ensure smooth traffic, safety, visibility, access, and security. While mapping all the areas of the museum where crowds might funnel into lines, think how you might use those bottlenecks to inform, entertain, and even sell.

LINES BEHIND THE DOCENT

One place people string out is behind the docent or tour guide, often block-ing other visitors, sometimes blocking independent visitors. If you have a group that's stalled, get them to talk to each other; it's pedagogically sound and creates a bonding that's the root of loyalty. Think about the frustrated lines behind the ropes in historic houses; turning the wait into a conversation is a natural for "houseguests." This exchange of ideas is used all the time in school tours, and I've often wondered why the same experience isn't offered to adults. Simply widening access to 360-degree viewing around free-stand-ing exhibits achieves a similar camaraderie: instead of a line, you've created a cluster, a conversation group. Another proven crowd-management technique is the handout, a staple of the conference room and classroom and a boon to museums. Docents and guides can distribute photocopies of other works by the artist or text to complement the guide's information. And the written word as an extension of the spoken word may salvage the 30 percent of the group that, expert say, learns better by reading than by hearing.

TOUR STARTING POINT

During the wait for tours to start, there's another opportunity to engage visi-tors in the museum as an entity. Some docents encourage visitors to exchange ideas with each other as they gather before the tour, and the docent timetable should include arrival at the starting point at least five minutes ahead of time. Having this museum representative in the lobby also encourages nontourers to ask questions and see the human face of your hospitality. The little cluster that forms around the tour starting point has a bandwagon effect that draws crowds into voluntary waiting groups. Not all people will stick with a tour, but the few minutes spent in the line opens a line of communication with them. The tour starting point is also a good place to provide a brochure rack or standing sign so that tourers can read while waiting.

THE LOBBY: WAIT AND SEE

Even without popular shows, lines form in the lobby: lines for tickets, the coat check, and the tours. Lobby value is a topic worth a whole book, for it is here at the introduction to the visit that visitors look around and get their bear-ings. In the lobby lines, visitors can learn about the exhibits ahead and, more important, pick up some pointers on museumgoing in general. For many visitors, the museum is an unknown challenge. It may be the gently exhilarating challenge of a new show in a favorite institution, but at the opposite pole it may be the supreme intimidation of a first-time cultural encounter. Focus groups among college students, for instance, reveal a dearth of museumgoing skills. Many have not been in a museum since the grammar school field trip, many more believe (sometimes erroneously) that none of their friends go to museums, and quite a few admit, reluctantly, that museums are for well-dressed, "cultured" people, not them. It is in the crowded lobby that the timid can look around and find people just like themselves and then observe how they navigate the museum trip.

TAGALONGS AND GO-WITHS

Then there is that large and anonymous market segment that swells any line: the visitor's companion. A museum may know a lot about target audiences who proactively choose to visit a museum regardless of the lines, but there is much less data on the visitor who gets dragged along with them. The visitors who planned the trip, not the accompaniers, are the ones who complete visitor surveys. Whatever the motivations of the person who tags along with "my girlfriend," whatever the thoughts of the young adult who accompanies "my Mom who thought it would be a fun for me," these go-withs need encouragement, especially if they are stuck in a line not of their choosing. They are prospective repeaters, members, and even donors. They have heretofore slipped past your promotions but now are actually in your establishment, trying the product. Now's your chance to develop this new prospect, and, fortuitously, they are a temporarily captive prospect because they're in that line.

The lobby wait is also an opportunity to promote and brand the whole museum. A line is simply a line, a generic event that happens at all manner of culture and leisure venues—until you turn it into something distinctive. A line at your museum can be a brief immersion in everything you stand for, the whole story of the experience beyond the lobby, not to mention the specific event they are standing in line for. Banners and panels behind the ticket counter announce upcoming exhibitions and events, suggest facilities for rental, and encourage membership. Obviously, this gives crowds something to read while they're waiting, an amenity deployed eons ago by grocery stores and movie theaters, among others. More important, these written documents also help define the museum and complete its identity. As visuals, these lobby graphics have the force of large size and primogeniture; they are the first thing visitors see. They also can provide ideas and up-to-the-minute facts that information desk personnel and tour guides can't or shouldn't. With overhead panels, it's easy to alternate from membership information to the size of the wedding venue to the next speaker on the lecture series. Flat-screen videos, playing appropriate videos or slide shows, are a good option for museums of any size; this familiar technology is used to ease the waiting times of visitors in retail establishments ranging from manicure salons to car dealer service centers. For museums, the expense might be off-putting, but the video can be repurposed for outreach programs and convention and tourism promotions.

Don't forget the often overlooked donor wall. People like reading names because although they may not know the owners, they see similarities to themselves. A well-designed recognition wall reinforces the mission and is almost an exhibit in itself. A shining example is the Tamastslikt Cultural Institute museum, owned and operated by the Umatilla Confederated Tribes in Pendleton, Oregon. This donor wall spans a swath of lobby and utilizes depictions of the coyote, the salmon, and the horse, symbols of the environment that are a museum-wide leitmotif. Donor names are inscribed in a panorama of leaping silvery salmon. If one wandered uninformed into this exquisite museum, its mission would be immediately and poignantly evident.

RESTAURANT WAITING AREAS

Other places where lines form and the crowd phenomenon occur can also be leveraged. Consider the bunching at the entrance to the restaurant as people gather for the next event: expectant, social, and having fun. Look on the lines at the audio rental counter as an audience waiting for the speaker. Capitalize on this mood of expectation with photographs of the exhibition, maps of the galleries, or promotions for partners in the community. I recall a seating area outside a museum restaurant where a dozen individuals were waiting for their respective lunch party to arrive. You could tell that they were in a good mood, but there was nothing to read, nothing to build on that mood of anticipation, and a productive downtime was wasted. The same dead zones also surround restrooms, the store, elevators, and the coatroom. Realize that younger people, particularly, are accustomed to multiple stimuli and thrive on what seems to others a cacophony of images. They abhor a vacuum, and you have so many ways to fill it.

The one beacon in a sea of uncertain waiting is the guard, that uniformed, official-seeming person to whom visitors turn for information and reassurance. These members of your museum family can make the wait less onerous by providing explanations, reassurance, or corollary information to fill the time. As James Cuno, director of the Art Institute of Chicago, says, everything in the museum represents its mission, from "the museum shop to our Web presence to our graphic identity to our publications to our exhibitions to how our guards greet you when you arrive." Whether that's what your administration planned for the guard staff, information about your museum is what visitors expect.

DRILL-DOWN

Even though both observation and anecdote indicate that lines are less problematic than once thought, things change. Here are some variables: your location, the size of the waiting area, and the nature of your customer. With diversification and global appeal, the cultural orientation of your visitor will change. The Utah Natural History Museum identifies three new groups of visitors attracted by events in Utah that have nothing to do with the museum: a major medical research facility nearby brings in scientists, the value of the dollar brings in foreign skiers, and a new hiking trail that passes the front door brings in outdoors people. Will new audiences like these have different attitudes to those of your current visitors? Will they require short lines? If observational research teaches anything, it's the importance of adaptability to the ever-changing behaviors of human beings.

Two types of research that you might conduct to probe more deeply into visitors' attitudes toward lines and waits are discussed next.

INTERNET SURVEYS

If your website includes information about a special exhibition, one likely to attract new and out-of-town visitors, a short questionnaire linked to the special exhibition page might say the following:

Thank you for your interest in our schedule of special exhibitions. To help us ensure visitor satisfaction at large shows, please tell us:

How long do you expect to wait for admittance to an exhibition?

- 5 minutes
- 10 minutes
- 15 minutes
- Other

How long a wait would be unacceptable?

Do you prefer a timed ticket rather than waiting in line?

- Yes
- No

If you knew there would be a wait, would you change any of these plans?

- Bringing children
- Bringing older friends or relatives
- Including lunch at the museum
- Stopping at the museum store
- Spending less time in other parts of the museum

An online survey has the advantage of convenience for the respondent, ease of data collection for you, and a broad sample of participants. The disadvantage is the inclusion of unqualified respondents with an uncertain history of or interest in museums.

TABLE TENT QUESTIONNAIRE

If your museum has an area where people sit down at a table, at the restaurant or reading room, your questionnaire could add some open-ended questions to the previous ones:

While you're relaxing, please take a few minutes to help us plan your visit to our upcoming exhibition:

Since there might be timed admissions, what other parts of the museum would you visit?

How long a wait would be unacceptable?

When you must wait, would you rather be with a friend or alone?

How can we help make a wait easier (e.g., seating, reading material, or videos)?

What time of day or day of the week would you be willing to visit to avoid lines?

- 9:30 A.M.
- 4:30 P.M.
- 6:00 P.M.
- Weekdays
- Saturday
- Sunday

If one day were set aside for members only, guaranteeing no wait in line, would you be willing to visit on that specific date?

- Yes
- No

Comments _____

This type of research has the advantage of a defined target: visitors already familiar with your museum who are engaged enough to spend additional time for food, relaxation, or learning. As with many forms of research, it not only asks for feedback but also gives information, a friendly and effective form of advertising. And it promotes membership.

SMILING IN OTHER CULTURES

Here's a third kind of research, essential for museums in a diverse environment: read up on nonverbal communication. The reality is that expressive faces do not occur equally in all cultures, with some cultures being considerably more facially emotive than others. Tolerance for lines and waiting varies around the world, and impatience is displayed differently, too. Even more stymieing is when and in what situations different cultures allow their people to show pleasure or discontent. LaRay Barna (1998) warns about the myth of similarity and advises researchers to not read their own emotions into the expressions of others. All cultures may dress alike, speak English, and use similar greetings, but beyond these similarities lies a world of differences. Schools, hotels, and hospitals in your community probably confront these diversity issues daily, and comparing your customer experiences would benefit all parties. In this case, the research could be as simple as a two-hour meeting for sharing ideas.

Observational research may start with 100 smiles and burgeon outward into ideas ad infinitum. If you're lucky enough to bump into a pleasant surprise, your work has just begun.

15

Queue-Less in the Lobby

A corollary to patient standers in queues is the queue-less. These are not impatient visitors but, rather, independent ones who will stand off to the side, wander around, or miss the lines altogether. They don't cut in line; they cut to the nearest free space. Some exhibitions, for example, lay out a path for visitors, but the queue-less find another route. Some diners wait in line for the café to open at 11:30 A.M.; others explore other areas until the line clears. Children on field trips who think museums are for exploration are particularly frustrated: they're forced to stick to someone else's trail.

Sometimes the queue-less ones are simply crowd avoiders: they need their own space. Observe the solitary figure the middle of the floor, gazing around the lobby. Look at the people in the cash register line who stand apart. Watch the visitors at the edges of the tour group clusters. These visitors want information but don't like clamoring for it. They're willing to wait for a table or to make a purchase, but they dislike the closeness of a cluster. You can see from their body language, even if you haven't studied proxemics, the people who want their space, who act and react with varying degrees of aloofness when suddenly enclosed in a strange, new environment.

These independent roamers, the nonlinear explorers who cover your space at their own pace and range freely along their own routes, don't present much of a problem. They love the freedom of a museum and know how to maximize your offerings. The crowd averse don't need much more help, and you already have methods for minimizing space crunches. Your real challenge is the truly clueless, the ones who just don't get it. They can't get their bearings. They don't get the point of an exhibition. They can't get comfortable. This free-floating group might get discouraged, never to return again.

ORIENTATION AND ACCLIMATION IN THE LOBBY

It all comes down to the lobby: the first place and the main place where the challenges of the independent, crowd-averse, and confused visitor can be addressed. For all the queue-less, the lobby promises relief. This open, neutral space is where the process of engagement begins. The lobby plays a large role in "framing visitors' opinions about the museum long before they [see] the first work of art." This aperçu comes from the Icelandic-Danish artist Olafur Eliasson, who consulted with the Hirshhorn Museum and Sculpture Garden in Washington, D.C., about its nongallery public spaces. The lobby becomes an orientation and acclimation area, not just a funnel for ticket transactions, information, and crowd control. Visitors can glimpse what lies ahead, watch where other people go, and read about the exhibits. It's like a book cover and table of contents. The queue-less, however, don't necessarily start with chapter 1, and they require guidance throughout the museum.

Fortunately, when you see disengaged visitors in the lobby, you can do something about it; unlike the disinterested consumers who never even give a museum a chance, you have clue-seeking visitors in hand and can guide them along. It's an opportunity to impress them with the distinctiveness of your museum, to win a friend.

OASES

Develop small oases where the lone visitors can get relief. The solo visitors may spend even more time than groups do, touring your museum. They simply want to gather information on their own rather than hearing it from a guide. Brochure racks or even pegs with information cards provide information to people who don't like structured tours. And your guides can help. Provide them with handouts or laminated information sheets to give to those who want information but don't like to stick with the group. Supply your guards with the same information handouts and a little training in addition. They will be the first person to whom the clueless wanderer turns.

MEDIUM AND MESSAGE

The queue-less turn up in unexpected places, needing information, so think about the store, coat check, restaurant, restrooms, elevators, and parking lot as stops along their journey of discovery. The various tools used in the lobby or galleries can be repurposed, and you will find that the medium, as well as the message, enhances their learning and comfort level. Just as college orientations aid students in absorbing their new studies, museum orientation spaces enhance the learning in the galleries. To continue the college analogy, new college research stresses the differences in student learning styles. Students learn by seeing, hearing, reading, and doing, in varying proportions. Some of the wanderers in our museums may simply be seeking a different kind of learning.

THE STICKERS

People on benches represent a smaller but more pressing queue-less problem. They may not be standing, but they still dislike being part of a crowd. Yet these are valuable customers because they are stickers. They either have been through your museum and are reflecting or are gearing up for it and planning. They may be waiting for a friend or looking at their store purchases. Whatever their reasons for sitting, they are reflecting on their experience, and the first thing you want is that they reflect pleasurably. The last thing you want is for them to move on, toward the galleries or toward the street, tired and cranky. So observe the woman sitting on a bench. Another woman sits on the same bench but not too close. According to Knapp and Hall (1999), women don't like to be crowded laterally by strangers, a behavioral reality that bodes ill for a museum with a small number of benches and a large number of visitors. Perhaps you should invest in reading tables at points throughout the museum or in more chairs (but not benches) or folding chairs to be brought out as needed. The simple solution is more seating, and if budgets give you pause, realize that people who want to sink in solitude for a few moments won't care what the chair looks like.

THE SOLO COLLEGE STUDENT

At the other end of the spectrum from the seasoned visitor is the greenhorn. You can spot the newbie by the unconfident slouch, the panicked eye, and the aimless staring around. In many cases, this is a college student on an assignment who has summoned the courage to come in alone. Focus groups will sometimes reveal that young people think museums aren't for them, that art museums are only for the well dressed and intellectual, and that history museums are still boring even ten years after the fourth-grade field trip. If you listen to this research, you will wring your hands, call in the consultants, and get nowhere fast. For although there are several good ways to bring in college students, a more immediate problem is how to make them welcome once they're inside. What observation makes lucidly apparent that focus groups and surveys do not is the frustration of not having enough information. The college student of the new millennium needs facts, outlines, and written assurance. Whatever other means of learning he or she utilizes—including visuals, team projects, and taking notes in lectures—the precision of the written word is important. Another behavioral habit of today's college student is his or her cell phone lifeline to mom and dad. Millennials don't mind wandering around solo because help is always at hand. And they expect that from you, too.

BEFORE AND AFTER

A fascinating lesson in familiarization occurred one bright weekday morning outside a museum where the tour bus had just disgorged thirty students whom the teacher was forming into groups. She worked haltingly, mixing and matching students with painstaking deliberation. And the students stood quietly, involved in this prepping operation. As it turned out, the teacher was assigning them to study groups, each of which toured with a different docent for their time in the museum. I watched as some groups sat on the floor and talked. Some gathered around the exhibits. Some listened. The individual approaches were palpable, and the students seemed engrossed. I bet they liked being individually placed in discreet groups, for whatever reason, and then treated in different ways as they journeyed through the galleries. They had been treated individually, briefed, and talked to in small-group settings, all learning techniques designed to make the learner feel comfortable and prepared to absorb new ideas. Other pretour orientations—in-class preview lessons or on-site videos—are commonly used, but I have never seen an actual before-and-after process. You have to observe the eager attention by the students to realize the strength of individual teaching.

There are similar techniques for acclimating adult visitors. At the beginning of guided tours, some guides ask visitors where they come from. It's a polite question with the power of individuality and context: visitors appreciate individual treatment, and they can relate the new museum to the ones back home. When visitors purchase tickets, the ticket sellers can ask for a hometown. It's a good field to add to the marketing database, and it also personalizes the experience for the visitor.

Museums succeed, flourish, and grow by retaining visitors. Everyone who walks in as a stranger should leave as a friend. It requires more effort to embrace the independent, the loner, and the wanderer; face it, they're moving targets and are not natural joiners. However, their mode of learning and enjoyment works perfectly for them, and they will find their own ways to connect loyally with your museum.

16

Frail and Hardy

On a beautiful day in June, as cheerful people strolled in steady streams past the large city-center museum, more than a few people stood out because they stood unsteadily. These were people on canes, walkers, or the arm of a stronger friend, walking slowly and perhaps exhaustingly but making the journey up the steps to the museum nonetheless. They must have desired that visit very much.

Glorious summer days, when the weather is inviting, when there is time for leisurely caring, may not be the best time to make projectable observations, but there is no mistaking the fact that a large number of frail people soldier upstairs and across hard floors to visit museums. The numbers might surprise you because they never show up on a survey. They aren't handicapped or in a wheelchair. They may not be old. One trait they share is determination, and that is a consumer attitude worth learning about.

This large cohort is important to museums because its members have free time, motivation, probably a higher-than-average education level, and possibly disposable income. It's a growth market segment in itself, separate from the more expectable segments of those over age sixty-five, retired, or visiting with grandchildren.

SMART AND INFLUENTIAL

Call this admittedly small cohort the "frail segment" and think about what they need and like. Obviously, they will need seats that are easy to get in and out of. They like nonslippery floors and convenient restrooms. Snack areas or a café would be nice because this is quite a trip for them; it might last several hours and it's extra work to then go out for lunch. They like learning and expect exhibitions that deliver a superior learning experience. They might appreciate the added erudition of a docent or educational brochure. They need the sense that they won't be crowded or rushed. Of course, you may be providing all these amenities already. And if not, it's admittedly difficult to provide them ad hoc for those who need them. But you can alert your staff to be sensitive to people on canes and walkers and be ready with a chair, attentive service in the store or café, or help with a dropped scarf. Attentiveness is the key because there's more to this segment than meets the eye at first glance.

Consider the influence that the frail segment wields over their family and friends. Frequently, it is adult children who accompany them to a favorite museum, and this busy sandwich generation is an audience that you may not currently attract. When they accompany their mobility-challenged (not handicapped) parent to a museum, they are reintroduced to sights and experiences they might not have visited since their own children were young. One middle-aged man—still working at prime capacity, much involved in his community, and the ideal demographic for cultural institutions—notes that the one time he sets aside for museums is when he visits his mother because it's an experience they always enjoy together. When you look at that special segment that accompanies a frail relative, you have an opportunity to capture a visitor you've missed with other targeted efforts.

Another group of people influenced by the museumgoing frail are their peers who share many active endeavors. There is a significant percentage of people who demographically are over age sixty-five and who are also demographically upper income and educated. They belong to a psychographic group of doers and possibly shakers whose energy is only somewhat compromised by physical weakness. They have time to meet for lunch, support the arts, and spread considerable buzz for your institution. They attend exhibitions and special programs. They fill the galleries and lecture halls at times when other groups are absent. When new, edgy programs are introduced, this group checks them out. Avant-garde has been happening in their lives for a long time, and they don't fear wasting their time.

One deficiency of the frail segment bears investigation, and it's hard to observe. Hearing loss affects untold numbers of people, some of whom scarcely notice it themselves. It affects museums in how you give information, guide tours, stage lectures and performances, and collect money at checkout counters. The result of bad hearing is not a physical accident or a restriction of activity but rather a subtle accumulation of poor communications—in the lobby, café, store, or guided tour—that diminishes the experience little by little. The problem goes away when you train your staff to speak up, slowly and clearly. People with more pronounced hearing problems might prefer audio tours because they are professionally narrated and can be replayed. Larger label type, more signs, and other visual aids help compensate for aural insufficiency.

WELL-CONNECTED DIGERATI

Just as you can't see the frail segment struggle to hear, you may not see how proficient they are in other areas. Throw out the persistent and pernicious image of a grandmother rocking on the front porch and replace it with granny on the Internet. Word of mouth, that robust new advertising tool made popular by social websites and blogs, is well known to the frail segment. These individuals are curious, highly motivated, and socially and professionally connected to wide circles of colleagues, friends, and family. They use the Internet for e-mail, searches, and a lot of photography. Many studies show an increasingly large percentage of Internet usage among older people and those at home. And here's a cautionary lesson in research: a 2008 poll of people who spend one hour or more on the Internet has crunched the numbers into groups, such as unmarried, nonworking, income over $75,000, and over age sixty-five. The group we're considering falls into all these categories, and to characterize them only as seniors does everyone a disservice.

DRILL-DOWN: EMPATHY SESSION AND AGING SUITS

More observation is necessary, and several corporate marketers and designers provide good models. Manufacturers of kitchen appliances and bathrooms are looking harder at baby boomers who, while not in any way disabled, are beginning to ache in different ways. General Electric (GE) is taking notes on what they do to see if there are behaviors that happen more than once. In GE "empathy sessions," young designers stuffed cotton in their ears, wore special glasses and rubber gloves, and put dried corn kernels in their shoes so that they could feel what it's like to be a consumer with challenged eyesight and hearing, a creaky back, stiff-jointed fingers, and aching feet. At Nissan Motor Company, employees wear an "aging suit" to feel what it's like to move with unsupple joints, poor balance, and aging vision.

This is not engineering for the handicapped mandated by the Americans with Disabilities Act (ADA) but rather a realization that older people don't hear dinging washing machine timers any better than they might hear a docent, can't read the dishwasher LED displays any better than they can read a label, can't stoop to get food out of the oven any more easily than they reach down for a cafeteria tray, can't push tiny buttons such as those found on coffeemakers or audio tour controls, and simply can't walk as far as they used to.

If you are an ADA museum, perhaps your staffers have already toured the galleries in a wheelchair simply to get the disabled person's perspective on exhibit sight lines and label height. What you need now is a newer, more subtle kind of research that takes you inside the body of an abled person who is just a little more fragile.

DRILL-DOWN: FOCUS GROUPS

Focus groups will provide more insights, and these might be easier to assemble than those targeting younger people. You don't have to tell them the subject is older people. They'll tell you themselves once they get together. Simply say that you are interested in their thoughts about the museum in the twenty-first century. To recruit a group of the frail segment, first look to your member list for those who joined, say, before 1975. Then look at donors at higher levels. You can also identify older people by the kinds or amount of purchases made at the store. Then mail or e-mail them an invitation to join a focus group on envisioning the future. Your goal is a focus group of eight to ten people. Start by asking them general questions about your hours, collection, exhibitions, programs, prices, and service. Older people will volunteer the age issues. They indeed are active and undaunted, but their self-knowledge is high, and they aren't shy about articulating what they need.

Following are some sample questions to ask the frail segment groups. Elicit further answers to any of them by using "prompts," such as: How does this apply to our collection, particular exhibits, special exhibitions, educational programs, lectures, events, galas, travel and tours, volunteer opportunities, discount promotions, prices, service, restaurant or café, museum store, reputation, image, and mission? This is a lengthy list of prompts and is viable because you have recruited loyal members or visitors who have demonstrated deep involvement with the institution:

When do you visit our museum? Do you prefer certain days or times of day?

Who accompanies you?

Do you wait for special exhibitions?

Thinking of just your friends, what aspects of our museum appeals to them?

What aspects of our museum don't they like so much?

Do members of your family accompany you to the museum?

What interests them?

Do they share your interests?

You've been aware of or involved in our museum for some time. What has changed, good or bad?

Considering other museums you visit or have visited, how does ours differ?

If you could change one thing, what would it be?

At this point, as you revel in the amount of expert consultation you can expect, you might wonder if the frail segment will turn out for a focus group. Yes, they will. Observation at a variety of lectures and enrichment programs, some early in the morning and some in very nasty weather, proves that the frail segment shows up in force, speaks with intelligence, and brings friends. Make the most of this valuable resource.

What the Guards See

The wine-and-cheese opening sparkled with conversation and intense viewing. The party honored a museum's ideal audience: members. Members trade up to higher levels, such as donors and sponsors; they are ambassadors of goodwill, and the museum was thanking them. To further nurture the guests, docents wearing name tags that said "ask me" roamed the rooms to answer any questions. It was surprising to observe that the guests asked "them": the guards. It was as if the docents weren't even there; most likely, they fit in too well, looked too much like the visitors themselves, and therefore might be too judgmental. The guards, on the other hand, exuded another kind of security: an anonymous assurance that the visitor's lack of knowledge would be safe.

At another museum, the scene is more mundane, a large, busy lobby pulsing with the routine number of visitors flowing around a large, circular information desk that is manned by five pleasantly dressed women and as many computers. Again, a strangely high percentage of visitors bypass the civilian booth and ask questions of the guards taking tickets. Many visitors stop and talk to the guards on their way out. Guards seem to be the go-to people everywhere. Especially when dressed in uniform, they are the employees whom visitors talk to.

There are two research projects here: why do information-hungry people prefer to ask uniformed guards rather than the folks like us at information desks, and what do your on-the-ground employees hear and see that you should know about?

Regarding the first issue, undoubtedly, uniformed guards look official. They are close by and convenient. And they don't intimidate like the well-dressed doyenne volunteering at the front desk. You might uncover these visitor attitudes in focus groups, but another reason is more subtle. The guards serve as greeters and farewell senders, too. At the entrance, as in a strange home, the guards function as hosts. Whereas the information desk people function to solve problems and confront you with questions like "can I help you?," the guards at the gate simply say "thank you" for your ticket or nod you in. There's no question-and-answer session. At the end of the visit, when the visitor is now fully acclimated and brimming with enthusiasm, the guard is right there, and I have seen exiting visitors nod at them and say "thank you."

ASTUTE PERCEPTIONS

The second issue is a juicy one and ripe for some drill-down research. Whether your guards stand silent and watch or interact, they absorb a lot of impressions. They see everything. They become superb observers of human behavior. On my museum visits, I often spend a few moments chatting up the guards, and their perceptions are astute and vivid.

At an exhibit of human bones, I asked the guard how people reacted. "They're upset," said the guard, "like that one." While talking to me, the guard had noticed out of the corner of her eye a visitor step up to the exhibit, and I turned my head just in time to see the visitor draw up short, the horror still clear on her face. The guard had caught that visitor reaction immediately. "They prefer that gallery," the guard said, pointing across the hall, "because of its beauty." The guard also recognized aesthetics, either on her own account or because of the reaction of visitors—again, a dead-on insight from the person in uniform.

If ever museum administrators considered the guards as merely stoic, enforcers for hire, it's probably time to reconsider. Guards are sensitive to the people in their environment and seem to feel the vibe. Quite possibly they applied for this particular job because they like people watching. They certainly observe a wide range of behaviors and are in the galleries long enough and often enough to evaluate what they see in ways only the most costly research could replicate.

ARTICULATE AND EVALUATIVE

At the new Denver Art Museum, I asked a guard about the celebrated slanted walls and zigzag galleries and how visitors navigated through them. The guard then performed a modified pantomime of how people walk through the maze-like space, trying to decide which way to turn first. She was quite aware of the disorienting effect on visitors and then articulated the process in words.

At another museum, I was interested in an object, a cube made from re-cycled materials that was meant to be sat on. I continually stress the value of chairs as places to relax and refresh, so I asked the guard how many people actually sat down, how long they stayed, and if they talked to each other. Hardly anybody availed themselves of the seat, the guard said, especially men. Guards observe and assess and are fine sources of insight.

In other arts venues, the staff is similarly alert to their visitors. At the Goodman Theater in Chicago, servers at the snack bar related in great detail how couples could not decide what to eat or drink without conferring, at some length, with each other. And at the $4 cookie counter at Lyric Opera of Chicago, the attendant described the inefficient ways in which the lines formed. "That must be difficult for you," I commented. "Oh, no," she said, "I just love all the people." Note the geniality of the guards and staff mentioned here. Professional researchers are paid a lot to be pleasant and open minded. Your amateur observers come by it naturally and at no extra cost.

SOMEONE TO TALK TO

The ladies at the information desk are white, middle aged or older, with uneventful clothes and hairstyles, and they are very friendly and intelligent looking. The guards are older, frequently people of color, and they're dressed in gray, vaguely military uniforms. Their ranks are supplemented, farther back in the museum, with even older civilians of the front-desk variety and quasi guards. It's a reality that some of your guards are more approachable than your volunteers, and that portends a lot when you're trying so hard to retain visitors. You don't want your visitors to be merely satisfied; you want them fulfilled. You want them to feel like they've come home so that they will return, tell their friends, buy memberships, and donate money. Cordial interaction with the museum's people is essential, and most of your front-of-the-house people are guards.

The trust that visitors place in uniformed guards is counterintuitive. Studies conducted with college students show that young adults still remember field trips when the guard was the enemy, always telling them to slow down and not touch. Conventional wisdom suggests that many segments of the population dislike policemen and that many more segments simply ignore them. Yet in a museum, they are respected.

Your guards are not faceless, as evidenced by the smiles and chitchat at the end of the visit. In the lobby, as visitors exit, men and women alike held extended conversations with the guards, just like friends. As noted in another chapter, people who visit museums with a companion enter and leave in a chorus of conversation and animation, seemingly bursting with ideas they want to share. If they're alone, they want to talk to someone, and that someone is frequently a guard. At the store, a similar camaraderie occurs. Shoppers, in the euphoria of the emporium, compare notes and chat with each other, and if a friend isn't along, they talk to the salespeople. If visitors are looking for a simpatico ear, the guard is handy and willing.

ENTRANCE TO EXIT CARE

Some museums recognize the role that the official staffer plays and train them accordingly. At the McFadden-Ward House in Beaumont, Texas, a guard is stationed in the street that separates the mansion from the carriage house. It's only natural to thank this traffic guard and then to comment on the museum. And the visitor will get an informed answer, says the museum's director; it's part of the training. At the Norton Museum of Art in West Palm Beach, Florida, the guards will take you to your destination, whether it's the next gallery or the far-off lobby. These museums understand the importance of keeping a visitor comfortable from entrance to exit.

One of the most profoundly meaningful exit lines was delivered in the store of the Terra Museum when it was in its own building in Chicago. As the visitor stepped up to the checkout counter, the employee asked, "And what memory of the Terra Museum are you taking home with you today?"

One museum takes unusual measures to foster visitor–staff interaction. The Pulitzer Foundation in St. Louis, Missouri, encourages visitors to talk to the "guards" by omitting wall labels. If one wants to know anything about a work—the title, artist, date, medium, or the whole story of the exhibition—one must ask the docents who are positioned, standing, throughout the galleries. According to the museum, when questions are asked, conversations ensue. Visitors tend to ask rather complex questions when there's someone to answer them, and it often happens that others in the vicinity will join in. Those staffers are acquiring great visitor insights.

Pay particular attention to guards in the lobby because that's the place where visitors get their GPS started. Elaine Heumann-Gurian (2002), who speaks passionately about public spaces, says that visitors use the lobby to get acclimated, to study how others act in a museum. New or infrequent museumgoers often worry whether they're smart enough to enter the hallowed halls of a museum and whether they will make fools of themselves. Focus group participants have indicated they thought they had to be "dressed up" to go to a museum and were relieved to find people in the lobby dressed like them. In the lobby, all these first attitudes will be on display, and your guards will note them.

DRILL-DOWN: BRAINSTORMING WITH THE GUARDS

Do you wish you knew what your guards know? Ask them. For a deeper scan of visitor behavior, schedule a brainstorming session with your guards and ask them to talk about what they see. Some guiding questions might be the following:

What's the most common behavior you're seeing in our current exhibition?

What's the strangest thing you've seen a visitor do recently?

How can you tell if someone likes what he or she is looking at?

Can you distinguish new visitors from people who have been to our museum before?

At what exhibits do visitors spend the most time? Why?

What exhibits don't visitors like? What confuses them?

What questions do they ask?

For another staff perspective on visitor behavior, convene a focus group of your store personnel. As already mentioned, the familiarity of a store setting gets visitors talking. The merchandise they buy and ask questions about also indicates what they liked in the galleries and want to remember. The staff in your store is a storehouse of customer insight and, of all the staffers in the museum, sees more visitors more of the time. Because shoppers can be voluble about their likes and dislikes, even the smallest kiosk acts like a giant ear.

To manage and lead a business, the experts say, managers and leaders should spend no more than four hours a day in the office and the rest of their time out where the business actually happens. Fortunately for busy museum managers, you have many eyes and ears already out there.

The Folks from Kazakhstan and Other Global Changes

A tour guide at a major contemporary art museum recalls a tour that started with the visitors telling where they were from. The first person, a well-dressed fortyish woman, indicated her husband and said that they were from Kazakhstan. How global we are becoming, thought the guide, and then was nonplussed when another couple in the group responded: what a coincidence—we're from Kazakhstan, too. We live in an exciting global community, and people from around the globe are visiting our museums in surprising numbers. The Utah Natural History Museum sees an influx of foreigners who come to Utah for the skiing. A small Oklahoma history museum gets world travelers driving through the American West. The petting zoo at Miami Metrozoo attracts people of all ages from all over the world who have in common a desire to get up close to animals.

Their reasons for visiting your museum might be the usual ones—cultural enrichment, education, socialization, and sightseeing—as might their demographics and psychographics of age, income, degree of education, interests, and needs. But outward similarities camouflage cultural differences that can't always be observed. This chapter takes a different approach to observational research, observing not the world's people but rather the world's museums to see how they gear up for multicultural visitors. This chapter also explores areas in which cultural differences may hold sway and suggests traditional research tools for understanding them better.

OBSERVATION IN MUSEUMS AROUND THE GLOBE

Here are some observations of museums around the world whose policies may differ from yours and whose visitors' expectations you might want to consider.

Shanghai Museum

The gorgeously designed interior of this proud new institution uses a palette of browns and beiges. There's a lot of skilled woodwork and marble and diffused lighting. Many of the treasures are in freestanding glass display cases. Many of the visitors carry sophisticated cameras, and they set the lens against the glass cases and snap away at will. Is this different from the policy at your museum? In Shanghai, it seems to be expected.

Amsterdam Rijksmuseum

Labels are in three languages: Dutch, French, and English, and they know how many of their visitors speak English as a first or second language. Brochures at many museums now come in six or more languages, but which languages are used will be an evolving issue, as will translation of your labels.

Tate, Britain

The older sibling of the Tate family of museums encompasses the world of art, as any institution of the British Empire would. Its labels list not only the artist's birthplace but also country of residence, so the viewer gets a sense of the cultural environment that informs artists' ongoing work. The globe-spanning British know better than most that people move around and that creative people will be especially sensitive to the many-splendored palette of cultures.

All French Museums

President Nicolas Sarkozy decreed that in 2009 that museums in France would open their doors without cost to youths under age twenty-five and all schoolteachers. The widely accepted concept of free education and museums' role therein has been adapted by a leader who views museums as a major pillar in his rebuilding of France's global prestige.

Australian National Maritime Museum, Sydney

The Welcome Wall overlooking Darling Harbor honors immigrants who could reach Australia only by sea. This is one maritime museum whose mission is sociological rather than scientific, demonstrating how museums can craft a mission that distinguishes it from others in its category. A lobby kiosk holds a touch-screen computer where visitors can search their genealogy and add to it.

Musée du quai Branly, Paris

Prolific architect Jean Nouvel designed the ambitious "museum of man" with ramps instead of stairs and padded leather banquettes built into the ramp walls where visitors could sit and watch videos that document many of the exhibits. Expensive and showy? Yes. But it demonstrates an acknowledgment of the visitor's need to learn by hearing and seeing a "label" rather than just reading it and the concomitant need to sit down.

Catedral Nacional, San Jose, Costa Rica

Along the two long walls of the nave, a parade of large paintings depicting the life of Christ were accompanied by painted labels describing each scene. The paintings were high on the walls and dimly lit, yet the labels were designed to be read, and they could be. The church treated these objects as an exhibit and interpreted it accordingly. In many churches and perhaps some museums, it is assumed that visitors understand the cultural patrimony displayed there. In a global culture, nothing can be assumed.

Granted, large foreign museums have the money and clout to explore different—and big—ideas that other museums only dream about. Museums in other countries often receive funding unknown in the American economy, but while we are envying them, we can borrow from them, for they have been welcoming multiple cultures longer than museums in the United States have, and they have experiences to teach us.

IMPLICATIONS OF BEING OTHER CULTURED

The danger of not understanding other cultures flared up in a competitor to museums: Disneyland Paris. The mistakes it made spotlight the importance of understanding other cultures.

Sited just forty miles from Paris, Euro Disney, when it opened in 1992, expected to attract a huge urban Parisian audience, not to mention families from around western Europe. However, Disney misunderstood the culture of European vacations, which for generations have taken place in August, not throughout the year. Disney didn't realize that long weekend trips are not as common in European cultures as they are in the United States. It misapplied the American love for automobile trips to Europeans. It didn't do the basic observational research of looking around Europe and noticing dozens of real castles—unvisited—that looked just the Disney faux castle. It misjudged the European culture of spending money, which favors campsites and relatives over costly hotels and restaurants. It didn't understand the European culture of vacations.

That was then, and times (and Euro Disney) change. And that leisure experience is not the museum experience. But cultural attitudes in one area apply to human activity in other areas, so here are ten hot points that might have cultural implications for your museum.

Lectures

American lectures, frequently called by the more informal term "talk," frequently start with questions by the speaker like "How many of you have studied Darwin?" Many lecturers will ask about the makeup of the group: "Anyone here from outside the United States?" It's part of our feedback culture but not part of other people's cultures. Japanese professors, according to Sheila Ramsay (1998), simply give the facts and expect the listeners to form their own conclusions. This has ramifications for tour guides who, in accepted pedagogical format, ask a few preliminary questions of their visitors.

Asking Questions

In some cultures, asking questions is a sign of interest, intelligence, and respect. But in other cultures, it's disrespectful to question the speaker's knowledge. Think how your school programs should be structured.

Getting Close to Others

Americans (and other cultures) are used to proximity, and a sign of success in a museum is a lot of people, as much as the fire marshals will allow. This might not appeal to visitors, diners, shoppers, or event attendees from other cultures, a trait to consider when guiding tours, setting out dining tables, designing store layouts, or renting facilities. The field of kinesics—nonverbal communication and paralanguage—teaches that body language ranges along a continuum from the reserved movements of Asians and Native Americans to the more outgoing actions of Euro-Americans to the gregariousness of Greeks and Italians. And these are broad generalizations that cover a universe of nuanced gestures and subtle signals. As Edward Hall (1998) points out, in northern Europe, where personal space is not to be intruded on, if someone so much as brushes your coat sleeve, you'll get an apology.

Lining Up, Queuing, and Clustering

Americans form lines, but they get to choose which one. In the United Kingdom, there's one long queue, with no choice where to go but at the end. In some cultures, shoppers stand politely at the butcher counter, whereas in others, they swell to the front in a clamorous but time-honored system that works. Obviously, lines affect every part of your museum, from the coat check to the cafeteria to the restrooms. And while public behavior is quickly learned by adults, schoolchildren may not pick it up right away.

Multilingual Labels and Brochures

On the surface, translated materials would appear thoughtful and sophisticated. However, even if you offered 100 translations, you would still slight the dialects and regions of somebody. If there are even six different languages on the brochure rack, the printing costs skyrocket. When it comes to weighing a good thing against a good budget, it's time to weigh other options. More visual and video aids might be equally helpful. Many museums, here and abroad, are supplementing static exhibits with video interpretations.

Use of Time

Compare the American compulsion to be on time with the relaxed attitude of many cultures where lateness is expected. Contrast our linear style of finishing one conversation before embarking on another with the practice in other cultures of an employee waiting on a customer and turning away for many minutes to help another. Craig Storti (1999) distinguishes between "monochromic" and "polychromic" time: doing things one at a time or doing everything at once. It has implications for every aspect of your museum, from the information desk to the restaurant to complementary programming.

Pointing

Using hand gestures comes easily to docents and lecturers when indicating an important feature of an exhibit or describing a lifestyle activity from another era. Depending on the culture, it's not so advisable in talking to a person.

Children

A Japanese professor relates that one of the problems of McDonald's in Japan was the listing of children's menus above the counter because parents were unaccustomed to allowing their offspring so much choice. They thought that parents should exercise more control and feared that McDonald's was eroding that discipline. So much of our education includes empowering young people that we lose sight of children who learn in a more rote manner.

Money

Everyone thinks about, spends, saves, and uses money differently. This cultural time bomb should be remembered when planning promotions, store prices, and food service. Many cultures revere museums and feel honored to pay something for the privilege of visiting. Similarly, the price points of items in the museum store will appeal differently to diverse consumers, especially with fluctuating exchange rates.

Perception

All human beings perceive, but across almost any culture line, perception changes. When testing an interactive exhibit or the navigation of an exhibition, it would be instructive to compare results among different cultures.

Corporate Support

In the Milan Art Museum, in a hallway leading to a temporary exhibition, the logo of the sponsoring corporation was woven into the fabric of the carpet. In the video screens on seat backs at La Scala opera house in Milan, when the subtitles didn't appear, logos of corporate sponsors did. In seeking corporate funding, we try to strike a balance between fulfilling our missions and fulfilling our budgets. Yet as more overseas companies enter our economy and contribute to our arts organizations, museums need to understand how other countries do business. It ultimately affects how your visitors are served.

DRILL-DOWN: STAFF OBSERVATIONS

Start with your staff. The world of cultural behavior and attitudes is such a medley that you'll have to analyze it in small bits. In terms of observing behavior, first, ask your staff to make on-the-spot observations while the activity is fresh in their minds. It might be something as simple as how long foreign visitors spend in the restaurant or a more complex activity, such as their interactions with their children. How do you spot a foreign visitor? Many docents say that they can't detect foreign visitors unless they overhear them talking. You'll have to scan for other indicators, such as the language on the guidebook they're carrying. You'd be surprised how much information your guards collect; one art museum guard told me about visitors from Hungary. "How did you know they were from Hungary?" I asked him. "We were discussing Liszt," he said.

ONE-ON-ONE INTERVIEWS

A one-on-one interview might produce rich results and is worth the asking. At the end of a docent tour, if the guide has elicited hometowns, ask if the foreign visitor would be willing to share observations for fifteen minutes. While not all cultures are comfortable with interruptions of privacy, many value education enough to participate; they admire educators and defer to them. Be frank and get right to the point with questions like the following:

> How is this museum or other American museums different from ones in your country?
>
> Was this tour the right length?
>
> What features would appeal to your friends, business colleagues, children, and parents?
>
> What aspects of American museums are challenging to you?

As with all research, respect their privacy, stick to the stated time, and thank them profusely.

CROSS-CULTURAL PROGRAMS

For a deeper glimpse into other cultures, organize a cross-cultural program with your local elementary or middle schools. Develop a session or workshops that include exercises and discussions to get the different cultures talking to each other. This probably occurs regularly in schools, and a museum's contribution of visual stimuli augments the exploration. It's a way to reintroduce your museum to the education community and continue important culture dialogues.

Primarily, be sensitive to the reality that not everyone in American museums was born or lives in the United States. The misunderstandings were highlighted by an experience of a docent in an art museum that was exhibiting Andy Warhol's iconic *Jackie*. She realized that not all visitors might be Americans and that the younger ones especially might not recognize Jacqueline Kennedy Onassis, so she asked, "Do you know who this is?" And one young woman guessed, "Monica Lewinsky?"

19

Shout Out for the Library

The library that first alerted me to the deeper significance of museum stacks was one I had to climb four flights of stairs to reach. The Textile Museum in Washington, D.C., had such wonderful exhibits that the small library signs leading to a back stairwell were all the enticement I needed to see what else the museum had to offer. It was a warm place, with a welcoming librarian, and I wondered why this museum, like so many others, was opening libraries to the casual visitor. Librarian Mary Mallia told me, "There are so many museums and so much competition for people's time, we have to try harder." She could have written my introduction.

As it turns out, not only scholars but also schoolchildren, college undergraduates, and garden-variety visitors like the look and the feel of a library, with their calm spaces that promise so much learning. Libraries mirror our culture in their openness, and they respond magnificently to the way we live. They open early and close late. They allow talking. They have computer stations, comfy chairs, study rooms, and coffeepots. Some have fireplaces. The people behind the desk greet all questions with a smile and information. Visitors can receive their knowledge, much as they can in a museum, in a variety of formats, for the infinite variety of museum exhibits substitute books, DVDs, audio books, downloads, online databases, photographs, labels at the shelves and tables, archived material, lectures, and movies. Libraries entertain children, work with home schoolers on curricula, conduct book clubs for adults, and, in villages throughout the world, provide e-mail access. No wonder the library culture is beloved and that museums would want to embrace it.

The question for museum administrators is how to best fuse the learning, enrichment, and even sociability of libraries with the museum. If you're looking to establish or enhance a library, there are several types of research that will expand your thinking and hone the possibilities.

DRILL-DOWN

First, start observing the visitors to the bookshelves your museum already has: your bookstore. Note what books people pick up and how long they peruse them. Do they look at the visuals on the front cover or the written communications on the back? Try to get a sense of the kind of people who inhabit the shelves; of course, this is subjective, but people are wonderful subjects of conversation and grist for the follow-up discussions you'll have with your staff. Observe how long people spend with the books, whether they stand or sit, and whether they discuss the books with others or use the time for solitary inspection. Watch the children and the interaction between them and their parents. Scan carefully the looks on faces and the body language. As with all observation, keep your eyes and mind open and see what transpires.

For deeper drill-down, track what books visitors purchase and the dates; such data might reveal interest in a current exhibition or the degree of interest in certain topics in which your museum specializes. If possible, train the register staff to ask one or two questions that might extrapolate to a library:

- Did you find information you were looking for?
- Is this book for a course or personal research?
- Do you need more information on the subject covered by this book?
- If we provided seating here in the bookstore, would that appeal to you?
- Do you need information that one of our staff could provide?

The synergy between museums and libraries is vibrant, and many best practices are already shared, as exemplified by the guided tours offered by the new Salt Lake City, Utah, library. When it comes to helping your visitors learn, when you want to hold your visitors a little closer, there's a big competitive advantage in having a library tucked away in one of your wonderful corners.

20

Insights and the Performing Arts

Audiences of the performing arts follow their own sets of motivations and exhibit their own peculiar behaviors, and insight-driven museum marketers benefit immensely from observing consumers of all the arts.

As museum professionals observe their visitors, track their paths, and uncover their habits and eccentricities, they must also realize that there is a part of these people they don't know at all: the part that patronizes the other arts.

Yes, even your most loyal museum visitor, *especially* the loyal museum visitor, frequently spends considerable time, money, and passion on your competitors in the arts world: theaters, symphony, opera, ballet, and lecture hall. In addition, this person might be quite attached to these competitive cultural organizations, bringing friends, joining up as members, and even investing in their futures via donations. In some cases, theaters are part of the museum complex—but one with a mind of their own.

If you're a theater marketer, the next two chapters are really for you. They will discuss observations made at performing arts venues with the aim of throwing a brighter light on the theater visitor. The observations will help you understand your complex visitors and provide a broader understanding of the breadth of the market. The truth is that most performing arts marketers are still operating on outdated research techniques that reveal little more about the ticket holder than age, ZIP code, education, prior arts involvement, and "where they heard about us." Although some ask for opinions on everything from the quality of the performers to the attractiveness of the sets, audience research, so far, seldom plumbs the attitudes of the diverse throngs that fill row after row of houses in every city and town in the country. There is a huge need to better understand all arts audiences because the arts business is immense, competitive, and an influential sector of the economy.

Several cautions apply when studying the visitors and audiences of another art form. As you will see, theater audiences are rather different from the museum crowd, operagoers are different from symphony lovers, and people who like dance differ from those who like lectures. The habits and actions of one group are motivated by a complex set of social and personal needs that preclude easy generalizing. Sometimes, the way a theater ticket holder acts is *sui generis* and has nothing to do with how an opera buff thinks or responds. The invaluable individuality and uncompromised creativity of the arts are not fungible. And so the following chapters don't seek to generalize and certainly cannot characterize with any degree of expert accuracy the comparative motivations of any audience. But rigorous observation will reveal habits and attitudes that instigate dramatic conjectures. Whether these "sightings" turn out to be useful or merely provocative depends on how deeply you explore beneath the surface behavior. The best research unrolls with a series of follow-up activities: staff discussion, evaluation, further exploration, additional drill-down research, and possible quantification. A major benefit of observational research is that you can start and stop and pick up again when you have the time.

Think how carefully you want audiences to watch and listen to you. This time, watch and listen to them.

21

Velcroed at the Ticket Window

Forty-five minutes before curtain, the first thing one notices about the lobby of the Chicago Shakespeare Theater is how many people pick up tickets at the box office. In the run-up to showtime, over 50 people approached the ticket windows, about 10 percent of the house, and most of them were couples. In this or any theater, it means that a sizable number of the audience comes in direct contact with representatives of the theater. And, not only that, this ticket holder brings along a soul mate. For a few seconds, the theater has not only the decision maker within sound of its voice but also the person with whom that person shares the decision—more precisely, the person who shares the momentousness of the decision—because as one strides up to the window, the other hangs over his or her shoulder, physically joined in the transaction. The body language conveys one strong message: this theater decision has been made cooperatively, and it's serious. To these two people, the theater experience is so consequential that they start sharing the experience even at the mechanical end of the process; they enact a small drama even when giving their name and picking up the envelope.

This strange pas de deux, this Siamese-twin ticket-window waltz, is repeated at box offices everywhere. You'll see it at matinee and evening performances, symphony halls, lecture auditoriums, and museums. I even saw the ritual crammed into the four square feet of the Teatro Nacional de Costa Rica's tiny box office niche. And sometimes, when couples attend with other couples, the same bunching occurs, with foursomes all clustering around the person picking up the tickets.

"Couples" does not necessarily mean "old married couples," although they seem to be a large part of the theater-symphony-opera-lecture audience. Friends, colleagues, and relatives also plan, coordinate, and attend a theater-based event. They behave the same way, performing the theater equivalent of backseat driving.

It is singularly noteworthy that the couples seem more connected, actually shoulder to shoulder, at the point of purchase than they are during the performance. In the theater, they are intent on the performance; at the ticket booth, their attention is on themselves. Do we have the right date? The right time? And what dates are available for the next show? Although it's clearly a pleasant experience for both individuals, the joint transaction seems to demand teamwork. This makes sense because the decision involves not only price and seat location but also the date—and competing leisure activities, like every other item on one's agenda, is becoming increasingly difficult to squeeze in. The importance of coordinating schedules may not come as a surprise; the intensity of it is surprising. There's a lot of gravitas at point of purchase.

IMPLICATIONS: PERSONAL CONTACT, TWICE

Observe well this ticket-window behavior, for you've been given a gift. You have a chance to connect with good customers, face-to-face, at a moment when they are already deeply involved and inside your venue. This is a rare moment to interact with the customer as a person, not only as an "X" on a seating chart. Observations show that most of these people have arrived early; they look relaxed and friendly. They neither dash up to the counter nor sprint away from it. In fact, they chat briefly with the staff person behind the window. And they stay in the convivial lobby rather than head for the confinement of their seats. As it gets closer to curtain, those picking up tickets are rushed, but they still check their tickets; you have precious seconds to reinforce the purchase with at least a thank-you, a human connection.

A cardinal rule of marketing is that it's more efficient to keep the customer you have than to try to get a new one. So it makes sense to nurture these customers you have literally in the hand. They are vitally interested in the current ticket and possibly future ones. They want to know how long the show lasts, the timing of the intermission, and when the snack bar will be open. They are hungry for information, and you can be the friend who supplies it and feeds them a few other points as well. This is when an already contented customer can be urged along the path to loyalist. The ticket-window personnel can say a few words about the production and upcoming shows. The booth itself can display information and promotional materials. The ticket envelope can contain order forms.

After these involved couples leave the ticket booth, watch as they merge back into the warm flow of the lobby audience, business accomplished, minds open to the event that lies ahead. The lobby beckons as a welcoming place to bridge the passage from business to pleasure, from the dramas of the day to the theater inside. The lobby can provide chairs for discussion, signage for information, and more staff to answer questions. For those in the lobby who already have tickets, the ticket windows are a good place for them to saunter over and find something to read or people to talk to and perhaps make another purchase. Newer theaters and museums have multiple ticket windows, each one a private place where the ticket holder can talk to a theater expert.

LOBBY STAFF PLAY THEIR ROLE

As a service organization, theaters, like museums or concert halls, need to pay particular attention to the people who serve the customer. The staff behind the ticket windows needs to be knowledgeable, pleasant, and speedy. Most performing arts organizations do exemplary jobs of training. These aren't simply ticketing machines; they have expert information about the show, the performers, and the authors in addition to the prices and seating chart. Training could also prepare staff to answer questions about public transportation and nearby restaurants and to engage in small talk.

In planning how to staff the ticket counter, don't stop until after intermission. Intermission crowds bubble with enthusiasm, and couples are primed to place future orders and consider next season's subscription series. Staff members standing nearby would help promote future performances. When you think of the effort put into postperformance talks, when couples are pressed to agree on staying later, it makes sense to try a midperformance "talk," even a short one through or near the ticket window. The only times couples split are for the restroom lines. If ever there was a reason to finally distribute restroom space evenly, getting couples back together is it.

COUPLES AT INTERMISSION

Between acts, the couple phenomenon strikes again at the coffee and cookie counter. The servers I have talked to observe as acutely as any professional researchers, and they note a veritable mating dance of food ordering. One half of the couple will ask about the cookies, get an answer, and relay this to the other half of the couple, who, by the way, is only inches away. The dominant partner will give the order. Then the other half of the couple will ask the server a question, and then both halves of the couple will discuss the situation more fully with hand gestures. To corroborate this behavior, I observed a refreshment counter for the entire intermission. Couples huddle and consult at length, and you must be prepared for it if you want a happy interlude.

The servers I talked to said this drawn-out process plays havoc with their resources during a short intermission, and this is with only two kinds of coffee and three varieties of cookie; one can only imagine the congestion if there were a bigger menu. The time required to mediate between snacking twosomes undoubtedly affects how theater management might staff and orient the snack bar. Underlying customers' food-ordering decisions is the fundamental insight that people at the theater act jointly and cerebrally. In another chapter, I highlighted the behavior of museumgoers who walk arm in arm, talk nose to nose, and touch each other as they point out this exhibit or that. The theater collaboration is different. This is not the warm emotion but, rather, clearheaded deliberation. Nobody wants to make a mistake; all parties want to understand precisely what's involved, be it the date on the ticket, the length of performance, or the contents of a cookie.

This mind-set informs many aspects of the theatergoing experience, not only enjoyment of the production but also reading of the program, purchasing books and scripts, paying attention to magazine-style mailings, and responding to ever more complex subscription plans. You are serving people's right-brain needs.

ADDRESS BOTH HALVES OF THE COUPLE

Service, however, is just one part of the marketing mix, and the arts organization can utilize couples-at-the-ticket-counter insights to home in on other aspects of the product and its pricing, delivery, and its promotion. Realizing that theater decisions are made in unison, take a new look at the cost of two tickets and any promotions you might design. Since twosomes use the theater as a place to be with the other person, provide enough seats for talking and enough food and drink to satisfy two hungers. Upgrade your customer relationship management and think about mining data on both parties to the subscription. Ideally, you will have e-mail addresses for both and subscribing histories for both. And if your two people don't live together—a sure bet at Wednesday matinees where a glance at the house will reveal mostly women of a certain age—make sure that both members of the party get mailings, merchandise offers, and announcements of complementary programs at their individual addresses. Parenthetically, nothing is more off-putting for a long-time matinee subscriber than receiving a new customer telephone solicitation because the tickets are in the name of her sister-in-law.

Another aspect of marketing—advertising and promotion—is put on alert by the behavior at the ticket counter. Theater decisions are made collaboratively, and that behavior should be addressed in the advertising. Most newspaper ads for theater, concerts, opera, or lectures avoid using "you," and rightly so. An ad that banners "you'll love it" sounds like it's talking to a party of one.

You can also advertise to your party of two in the lobby, in the many minutes before the show or the fifteen minutes of intermission. Put those expensive magazines you send to series ticket holders out in the lobby for easy reading. There's time for it. If there's room in the lobby for video screens or even laptops, think of the extended story you could tell—not simply a clip from one scene but an infomercial and in the context and excitement of the theater itself.

DRILL-DOWN

To understand the couple dynamic, you might want to do one-on-one research and not simply another questionnaire. Here at the ticket booth is the chance to get audience information that questionnaires are inherently incapable of unearthing. Questionnaires are another form of paperwork, and the intricacy of envelope pickup is probably enough paperwork for one day. Questionnaires are typically completed by one person, not a couple acting in partnership. Theater surveys tend to be long and windy, asking about everything from customer habits to their critique of the scenery. However, the lobby gestalt seems more like a cocktail party than a seminar. So leave the in-depth questionnaire where it now resides, at the end of the performance, and use this opportunity for motivation insights. Conduct thirty-second research at the ticket window by having staffers ask these short questions:

Are the other dates on your subscription series satisfactory for both of you?

May I give you two some information on future performances?

I know it's hard to coordinate schedules, but was the exchange process convenient?

We have discounts for two at some nearby restaurants. Have you received them? Would you like the packet?

These questions may end up being mere niceties, but they are meant to elicit conversation, some indication of couples' attitudes toward the experience in general. Take a few seconds to listen to the responses. As with all research, the real advantages come when you discuss the responses in staff meetings. If you have time for only a few such intercepts, they will direct you down interesting paths. And politeness, even if it doesn't provide answers, always bears fruit.

COUPLES FOCUS GROUPS

Focus groups would illuminate the couple dynamic if you have the time and money to recruit for twosomes. The same difficulty two people have in deciding on a theater date precludes them from coordinating a focus groups session, but it's a beguiling idea; you see from the minute a married couple or two friends walk in the door how they act together. Throughout the discussion, their verbal and nonverbal interactions will amaze and enlighten you. After the preliminary introductions, ease into the discussion with questions such as the following:

When was the last time you attended a theater or concert performance? Describe it briefly.

What other live performances do you enjoy?

What's most important, price, seat, or date?

After the first five seconds, you'll see clearly how the couple interacts. You might want to probe these questions with "what else?" or "explain," and you'll open up a world of two-for-the-price-of-one insights. Or you can proceed to more couple-oriented topics:

Whom do you attend theater (symphony, opera, lecture series) with?

Who initiates the idea?

Thinking back over all your years of theatergoing, who was the best person to get tickets with?

What points do you agree on?

Where do you have trouble coordinating?

Do you ever go to the theater alone?

What do you talk about before the show?

What's your conversation like after the show?

How do you use the intermission?

If your regular theater companion couldn't make a performance, who would you ask instead? Who wouldn't you ask?

VERBATIM SURVEYS

The golden opportunity called "intermission" lets you field a hybrid kind of research—part survey, part focus group. Conduct it via lobby computers, which give respondents a chance to write verbatim and not simply check multiple choices. This method has several advantages: it reaches more people than focus groups can provide and much more economically, it's convenient for the respondents, and the privacy of the written word elicits more trustworthy information. In addition, writing answers is an intellectual process, and theatergoing with a companion involves the intellectual process of planning. And as an actress once told me, when a couple attends the theater, it's more analytical than emotional. You may not get many couples to huddle over a computer keyboard during intermission, but it's a diversion that, over a season, will amass a body of information. And, like all research, it will reinforce the experience for the participants.

Heed the variables of any research you conduct. Time of day will affect results, as will day of the week and time of the year. Different shows could strongly affect how couples answer questions, especially if they differ in their opinions of the content, the performers, the running time, or any of a dozen other reasons. Weather can dampen a couple's attitude irretrievably. And if one has had a bad day, the moods of two people will be affected. The chemistry of two people instead of one multiplies the variables incalculably. Expect insights, not answers, but expect plenty of them in duplicate.

22

The Upside of Intermission

The soaring, gilded lobby of the Civic Opera House in Chicago is an opera in itself. From the ornate balconies and the sweeping red-carpeted staircase, one can look over the main floor awash in color and swirling with activity. The air hums with chatter, and the ambience is thick with high spirits, goodwill, and the frisson of artistic moment. The ticket holder, having been swept in by gusts of air from the pillared entrance and then greeted by a ticket taker in resplendent greatcoat, feels a part of the show. Throughout the expanse of lobby, stairway, and balconies, people meet, sometimes by chance, and gather in groups to talk and laugh and stand and look at the passing parade. Before the show starts, the lobby is a show in itself. And after the first act, the show continues throughout intermission.

In theater lobbies less large and not so grand, in storefronts and school auditoriums, the mood is much the same: clustering, animated conversations, and socializing. Even people who come in pairs end up in foursomes. As at a cocktail party, they congregate and disperse. As if onstage, they move and turn, facing every direction as if to address every other being in the audience. Whatever the theater, symphony, opera, dance, or lecture, the sociability is palpable; any organization that wants to build a community would be gladdened.

Contrast this with the most inert, listless theater audiences in the history of performing arts: the ones entombed in their seats at intermission. At a given performance, 30 to 50 percent stay in their seats, reading the program cover to cover, checking their cell phones, desultorily talking to their companion, knitting, working a crossword puzzle, or just sitting. A dismaying number simply sit, looking irretrievably tired, trapped, or bored. When the lights come up and the actors depart, they seem helpless to act for themselves. But for most theater marketers, a splendid opportunity to retain and reinvigorate customers is missed.

IMPLICATIONS OF STAYING PUT

A significant number of your visitors, people who have taken the first steps of choosing a performance, reserving seats, and traveling to your theater, are now missing out on the audience development activities in your lobby. When they remain in their seats, they aren't going into the lobby to socialize, to read the informative panels, to buy food and gifts, to stand in line for the washroom (another social venue), or to bond with your institution. The sociability of the intermission merits special attention as the time for the collective audience to become individuals again, compare notes on the set design, ask each other questions about the plot, or comment on the performances. It's an essential interlude for memory making, much more powerful than the end of the show and the fatigued flurry of gathering belongings, finding the car keys, and going home.

Between acts, there's money to be made, if the lines at the snack bar are any indication. One can argue the profitability of snack service—and at many theaters coffee is free—but not the sociability of food or the reenergizing of a body that's been sitting in a dark space for an hour or more. Here's a place where people can chat with each other and, an untapped resource, with servers behind the counter. Part-time waitstaff in theaters are invariably friendly and often knowledgeable about your show. When they interact with customers, they bring the audience into the experience, converting them for a moment from viewers to reviewers. A simple "hope you're enjoying the performance" from a server as he or she hands over coffee and a cookie can do wonders for imprinting on the visitor's memory the glow from the stage. The revenue can be useful, too.

In many theaters today, even the smallest ones, a kiosk of souvenirs lets the audience browse and recall the sights and sounds from the performance. Large institutions with well-stocked stores are able to capture precurtain visitors and function not only as a profit center but also as the warm-up act. At the Ravinia music festival outside Chicago, concert-goers fill the park all summer; but there is plenty of warm-weather competition. A gift store and kiosk heighten the Ravinia experience at retail. Often, CDs of the evening's performers are sold, enhancing the evening after the music stops. When visitors travel long distances to your venue and spend many hours there, it's smart to reinforce their loyalty with appropriate merchandise. At the Shakespeare Repertory Theater in Chicago, a stunning reimagination of London's old Globe Theater and glorious views of Navy Pier and Chicago's shoreline are just part of the scintillating lobby scene. One out of three patrons browse the bookstall, often with a cup of coffee, sharpening their Shakespeare-sensitized wit with books and scripts of current, past, and future plays. These, along with logoed gift items, give bard lovers a memory to take away and share with family and friends. As with museum stores, purchases reinforce the message of the theater, bringing the experience home.

Many theaters use lobby displays, much as museums do, to further explain the show to the audience. Like a silent dramaturge, these exhibit panels put the play in context historically, socially, and politically. The job of a dramaturge has been described as helping the actors, set designers, and sound engineers understand the environment the playwright had in mind to better communicate the original intent. Lobby displays enhance meaning for the audience.

Other pleasant lobby diversions include television monitors in a suburban theater (used heavily one Super Bowl evening) and lockers at a theater in Lincoln Center (reducing the discomfort of having to sit on one's coat).

In many smaller theaters, there is no curtain, so scene changes and refurbishment take place in full sight, a behind-the-scenes look at the workings of a theater. Some theaters actually stage half-time entertainment, with bits of action onstage that enrich the story. These theaters do an excellent job of acculturating the audience to their unique ethos.

LONGTIME TICKET HOLDERS AND DONORS

Observation also shows one audience segment that merits special attention: seniors. We're talking about the older elderly, the large numbers of people in their late seventies to nineties whose healthier lives and financial resources take them to many corners of the arts world where they hold subscription series and donate generously. Older people don't have the same intermission outlets as their younger counterparts. They don't hear as well or chat as much; they don't stand comfortably in snack lines. Nor do they whip out cell phones. They seem to have the same conviviality as middle-aged audiences, although many come alone or with a less hardy companion, and bad weather does not seem to halt their progress. They could use some good lobby entertainment, though, because theater and concert outings are a big part of their social lives, and they make a day of it. As you build your databases, pay special attention to these loyal stalwarts. They have probably been subscription ticket holders for a long time, and you don't want to lose their patronage. Their range of leisure activities has narrowed, and they can lavish more of their financial resources on you. As for the younger audiences you plan to nurture, these elders excel as ambassadors to their younger relatives. Not-for-profit organizations point out that philanthropy flows from generation to generation, that parents introduce their children not only to the overall concept of philanthropy but to the specific recipients as well.

The donor wall has been mentioned in other chapters, and it probably gets read more during performance intermissions than any other time. This list of names is a verbal portrait of your audience, one that other theatergoers can view to get a sense of how many people belong to your theater family, who they are, how long they've been involved, and even the monetary value they place on your agenda. Donor walls don't have to be cast in bronze, as bronze is hard to read, but they should provide as good a read as the donor lists in your program. List your donors legibly, situate the wall in a place that's easy to gather around, and let this fund-raising device double as intermission entertainment.

There's another fruitful time, well before intermission, to reach your audience: the preperformance lecture. For example, on a Sunday matinee at the Chicago Symphony, over 200 people came to hear a conversation between a soloist in the upcoming performance and a local music columnist. Two hundred people equal one-tenth of the symphony hall's capacity. This is a significant group not only because of its numbers but also because of its defensive tactic. When attendees choose to spend an entire afternoon with you, forgoing your competitors in the leisure and arts arena, you're not only cementing a relationship but also preventing others from forming.

DRILL-DOWN: BEYOND THE SURPRISING FACTS

Steven Levitt and Stephen Dubner (2005) teach to look for surprising data, to be skeptical of the obvious facts, and to look beyond them and tease out what other meanings they might have. Their case studies are extreme examples of reading between the lines, and it's a good process to adapt when observing your audiences. The goal, then, after you have ascertained that many people stay in their seats during intermission, is to demand some explanation.

Since the seat stayers cover all ages and psychographics—readers to knitters to starers—several types of further research will yield answers. Focus groups are always useful because they screen for the right target audience and focus squarely on the issue at hand. It's conceivable that you could assemble an impromptu group from attendees the day of the performance among the people sitting in their seats with nothing to do. Another easy method is a survey, also distributed during intermission to the target audience. If you have a small, intimate theater, you could conduct short one-on-one interviews during the intermission.

Here are some questions to ask regardless of the research method:

During intermission, do you usually go to the lobby? Why?

What do you do during intermission (e.g., restroom, snack counter, bookstore, talk to friends, read about the performance, read about the actors, use my cell phone)?

If you don't leave your seat, why? (Maybe they don't want to leave their coats unguarded.)

Do you know what's available in our lobby?

What have you seen in other theater lobbies that might interest you?

Do you or anyone you know have disabilities that make leaving your seats difficult? Are there ways we could help?

If you stay at your seat, what do you do?

Do your intermission choices vary depending on the performance? The time? The season of the year? Explain.

Would you better appreciate your total experience if there were displays in the lobby that gave background information on the current or future performance schedule?

Whether you conduct a focus group, interview, or survey, pay attention to variables such as specific performance, time, and day of week. For example, people respond differently at an evening performance than they will at a weekend matinee. Weekday matinee audiences tend to be older and female. People who stay in their seats may have a higher level of interest in taking a survey than those who are standing in the lobby.

CONSUMER KNOWLEDGE AT THE BOOKSTORE

You would reach a different slice of the lobby crowd if you surveyed those at the bookstore, where patrons are browsing for knowledge and might be intrigued by sharing their stories. More theater education departments are setting up stalls in the lobby before, during, and after the show, and it would be efficient to leave a stack of questionnaires on the counter. Some sample questions are the following:

How many hours a month do you spend browsing in bookstores?

Do you ever study a play, opera, or symphony, the actual script, score, or lecture, before attending a performance? After the performance? At intermission, either by browsing through a book or buying?

When do you discuss plays with others? During intermission? Before the show? After the show? If after the show, how long does the play stay in your memory, and when might you talk about it?

Since there will be at least one staffer running the bookstall, have him or her ask a few friendly questions at the time of purchase. They might stimulate a conversation that could stoke future staff discussions on your audience. Some questions to ask are the following:

Is this a gift or for yourself?

Would you like to be on our mailing list for other theater books?

That [referring to specific book topic] is a wonderful play, isn't it?

Another form of research devolves from the bookstall: data from the register that can be analyzed for consumer insights. Information such as title of book, quantities bought by one purchaser, and time of purchase contains deep veins of insights that should be mined. People who buy books before the show might be more invested in learning, indicating the profitability of a lecture program or CDs. People who buy multiple copies may have like-minded friends who can be nurtured as prospects. People who buy a title other than one relating to the current production are probably theater junkies who can be courted for subscription series. As a retail marketing consultant says, "Retailers who have been collecting data and doing nothing with it need to get smart and strategic about understanding . . . customers."

NONVERBAL RESEARCH

A variation of the focus group is interventions, activities that go beyond moderator questions and mass group responses. Some audience members are not vocal. Some may not speak English well. Perhaps you're trying to develop a school program and want to conduct research with children. So instead of asking questions, the intervention disciples recommend having the participants draw their favorite theater activity. Another intervention activity involves showing photos of productions or of the performers and asking respondents to comment on them. Facilitating the first two research techniques might require training, but even a novice can learn the basics. The idea is simply to help participants find words to express their attitudes.

Behavior and motivation are the lifeblood of the theater, and in insight-driven marketing, it extends from the stage to the rows. Even if this observational research goes no further than discussions within your organization, you will be the richer for it.

Epilogue

In 2008, the Museum Association of New York (MANY), in the "Trends" section of its website, stated that a mere nine hours per year, per person, were spent engaged in cultural activities. It is incumbent on all museum professionals to look around and discern how and in what quantity visitors spend those precious hours in museums. MANY went on to caution about a second trend, the dearth of stability as upper management retires. So the future holds twin challenges of invisibility on the part of visitors and volatility on the part of management. Observational research cannot solve those problems, but it can open new windows in formerly monolithic walls. Changing behavior is a reality that has been occurring since humans segued from hunting and gathering to the wheel, and it will continue to affect visitors and management.

Observational research is a scary thing, always reminding you of things you didn't know. Every time you look around, there it lurks, forcing you to scratch your head and say, I didn't know that. It's disarming to realize that perfectly rational people behave in such surprising ways. And you'll never get accustomed to it; just when you're comfortable thinking outside the box, another box appears.

Once you observe how people go about their lives, you start down a path that keeps opening virgin territory. In the next five years, based on easy-to-see observations, those new territories include precision slicing of current market segments, cultural reorganization, new emphases on complementary programming, learning styles, and time fracturing. As culture leaders, museums must understand the forces behind the changes.

NEW SLICES OF OLD SEGMENTS

One slice off an old segment is the older consumer accompanied by middle-aged children. The two segments have been recognized for a long time, but the older people were marginalized, and the middle-aged were no longer defined as caregivers. Many other existing market segments can also be viewed in several ways, and here are a few more for future consideration. The field trip segment, once it leaves the museum, splits into children of nonvisiting adults, children of school board members, teachers with contacts in the community, and bus drivers with a whole new circle of possibilities. Many of these thin slices of old segments are created by cultural trends, and others can be forecasted simply by observing.

CULTURAL REGENERATION

A prevalent cultural reorganization is that of stay-at-home mom to nonmom caregiver. Look around at those caring for toddlers, and you'll see grandmothers, nannies, fathers, and grandfathers. Changes in American lifestyles have subtly invaded traditional market segments and given them a totally new look. When the caregivers gather at, say, the botanic garden, the group might include moms, salaried nannies, and grandmothers, all connected not by age, income, or background but by their caregiver role. Another culture modification is retired men who don't play golf but rather register for classes, volunteer, or work part time. As the globe contracts, other cultures will bring their evident habits and their subtle influences to our accustomed groups. And these will be carried not only in the backpacks of museum visitors but in the portfolios of museum administrators as well.

To understand the power of complementary programming, consider this observation. It was Super Bowl Sunday, and a large metropolitan art museum was empty, apocalyptically silent. Just downstairs, however, hundreds of people congregated, happily chatting, exhibiting the noise and color that had been drained from the galleries. These visitors had come for the theater performance, bringing in consumers of a different mind-set, not to mention prospective members and donors. Museums will probably always be based on collections and exhibitions, but their programs will provide important sources of revenue and adjunct channels for support and growth. There are all kinds of programs that attract new visitors and new support: another museum offers teacher continuing education and certification classes. A botanic garden offers yoga classes. Once you've observed their robustness, it will be hard to question whether to take the big step to a profit center.

LEARNING STYLES

Learning styles went under the microscope in the early years of the twenty-first century when colleges suddenly confronted the millennials. These were a new breed of student, overprotected by parents, underprepared by elementary education, and supercharged by the Internet. They learned fast and lost concentration fast, and they knew a little about everything but very little about other things. They expected a lot from life but not so much from their own effort. And they were very, very smart. They still are, and they are getting more so. Colleges have adapted to their varied and increasingly singular learning styles, and museums must, too. In a few years, when millennial students become millennial adults, museums will face the same challenges from members and donors. It takes practice to observe what people expect and how they are capable of absorbing it, and the skill is worth developing.

TIME SHIFTS

All observations take time, and time will fly asunder in the coming years. The concept of flextime was radical in its day, and the flexing continues. Visitors who used to listen intently for a sixty-minute tour now can appreciate your story in thirty. Meetings scheduled for two hours can be conducted in one and a half. Visitors for 10:00 A.M. openings are through with breakfast by 8:00 A.M. People who work all day and enjoy the arts at night are working longer and getting older and enjoying nighttime activities less. When you observe the unusual ways in which visitors use a museum, you realize that these eccentricities are really no more than creative time usage. Visitors who work on their computers in the museum, as if it were the library, are just changing the time and place of their study hall. Friends and relatives who linger over lunch in the café are not, of course, eating; they're making use of found time. When you see someone hurry through your galleries, don't dismiss it as disinterest; celebrate it as an affirmative choice in a day full of other options.

The transformations ahead—new management formulas, 360-degree vision, changing demographics and psychographics, and galloping diversity—will not be solved by professional guidelines and academic learning. Only original thinking can move fast enough to match cultural change. Visitors' lives, outside museums, progress with the speed of digital communications, the calendar, and life. Keeping abreast of consumer needs and styles starts by listening to them with your eyes as well as your ears. Keep watching with an open mind, and the next transitions will be exhilaratingly clear.

Bibliography

Ahmed, Azam. 2009. "Face That Launched a Thousand Products." *Chicago Tribune*, January 14, sec. 1, p. 19.

Allen, Sandra, and Michael Swidler. 2008. "The Millennial Student in Higher Education: Translating General Consumer Behavior to Specific Learning Behavior." Columbia College Chicago Faculty Retreat, August. First presented to European Institute of Retailing and Services Studies, Zagreb, Croatia, July 2008.

Anholt, Simon. 2006. *Competitive Identity: The New Brand Management for Nations, Cities and Regions.* Houndmills: Palgrave Macmillan.

Ariely, Dan. 2008. *Predictably Irrational: The Hidden Forces That Shape Our Decisions.* New York: HarperCollins.

Barna, LaRay M. 1998. "Stumbling Blocks in Intercultural Communication." In *Basic Concepts of Intercultural Communication*, edited by Michael J. Bennett. Yarmouth, ME: Intercultural Press, 173–89.

Behrens, Web. 2006. "What the Heck's a Dramaturg?" *Chicago Tribune*, February 19, sec. 7, p. 7. http://www.osha.gov/SLTC/etools/computerworkstations/ components_monitors.html (accessed January 19, 2009).

Bennett, Michael J. 1999. "Intercultural Communication: A Current Perspective." In *Basic Concepts of Intercultural Communication.* Yarmouth, ME: Intercultural Press, 19.

Black, Graham. 2005. *The Engaging Museum*. New York: Routledge.

Bloom, Julie. 2009. "Free Admission Plan for Museums in France." *New York Times*, January 14, sec. C, p. 2.

Brillat-Savarin, Jean-Anthelme. 1825. "Physiologie du Gout." http://www.amazon. fr/physiologie-du-go%C3%BBt-Jean-Anthelme-Brillat-Savarin/dp/2080811096 (accessed February 6, 2009).

Calvin, Heather. 2008. "Using Research to Make Strategic Decisions." Paper presented at the annual meeting of the American Association of Museums, April 30.

Chakrapani, Chuck. 2008. "From the Editor." *Marketing Research* 20, no. 4 (winter): 2.

Chronicle of Philanthropy. N.d. http://philanthropy.com.

Chung, James. 2007. "Reach Advisors Study of Family Visitation at Museums, Part II." http://www.reachadvisors.com (accessed August 24, 2007).

Clifton, Rita, et al., eds. 2004. *Brands and Branding (The Economist Series)*. Princeton, NJ: Bloomberg Press

Cova, Bernard. 1996. "The Post-Modern Explained to Managers: Implications for Marketing." *Business Horizons* 39, no. 6 (November/December): 15–23. http:// firstsearch.oclc (search: "Tribal Marketing").

Davis-Taylor, Laura. 2008. "Sustaining the Brand Experience: Managing Retail Evolution in an Era of Economic Challenge." *Marketing at Retail*, December, 6, 8–9.

Diamond, Jared. 1999. *Guns, Germs and Steel: The Fates of Human Societies*. New York: Norton.

Finkel, Jori. 2008. "A Man Who Loves Big Museums." *New York Times*, May 18, Arts section, p. 31.

Florida, Richard. 2004. *The Rise of the Creative Class*. New York: Basic Books.

Geissler, Gary L., Conway T. Rucks, and Steve W. Edison. 2006. "Understanding the Role of Service Convenience in Art Museum Marketing: An Exploratory Study." *Journal of Hospitality and Leisure Marketing* 14, no. 4 (April): 72.

Glader, Paul. 2008. "Home Appliances to Soothe the Aches of Aging Boomers." *Wall Street Journal*, December 3, Personal Journal, sec. D1, pp. 1, 6.

Golding, Emma. 2008. "Anthropological Marketing Insights: Why Non-Verbal Cues Are Crucial to Advertising Strategy and Design." In *The Why of the Buy: Consumer Behavior and Fashion Marketing*. New York: Fairchild Books, 357.

Goodwin, Doris Kearns. 2006. *Team of Rivals: The Political Genius of Abraham Lincoln*. New York: Simon & Schuster.

Hall, Edward T. 1998. "The Power of Hidden Differences." In *Basic Concepts of Intercultural Communication*, edited by Michael J. Bennett. Yarmouth, ME: Intercultural Press, 53–67.

Henderson, Naomi R. 2008. "Managing Interventions: Projective Techniques Get below Top-of-Mind Thinking." *Marketing Research* 20, no. 3 (fall): 44–46.

Heumann Gurion, Elaine. 2002. Speaker at the annual meeting of the American Association of Museums, May.

———. 2005. Panelist at the annual meeting of the American Association of Museums, April.

Holt, Jim. 2008. "Annals of Science: Numbers Guy." *The New Yorker*, March 3.

Horan, Nancy. 2008. Lecture, Wilmette (IL) Public Library, May 4.

Kannankutty, Nirmala. 2009. "Unemployment Rate of U.S. Scientists and Engineers Drops to Record Low 2.5% in 2006." http://www.nsf.gov/statistics/infbrief/nsf08305 (accessed January 31, 2009).

Katzenbach, Jon R., and Douglas K. Smith. 1997. *The Wisdom of Teams*. Boston: Harvard Business School Press.

Keen, David. 2008. "Using Research to Make Strategic Decisions." Paper presented at the annual meeting of the American Association of Museums, April 30.

Kennedy, Randy. 2008. "An Identity Crisis? Hirshhorn Embraces It." *New York Times*, May 10, Arts section, pp. 1, 21.

Knapp, Mark L., and Judith A. Hall. 1999. *Nonverbal Communication in Human Interaction*. 3rd ed. Austin, TX: Holt, Rinehart and Winston.

Levitt, Steven D., and Stephen J. Dubner. 2005. *Freakonomics: A Rogue Economist Explores the Hidden Side of Everything*. New York: William Morrow, an imprint of HarperCollins.

Liggio, Christine. 2008. E-mail on market segmentation. Pram-bounces@listserve.
com on behalf of Christine Liggio, February 13.

Loechner, Jack. 2008. "More Gray, More Affluent, More Internet Shopping." April 8.
http://www.mediapost.com/publications/index.cfm?fa=Articles.showArticle&art_a
id=80044&passFuseAction=PublicationsSearch.showSearchReslts&art_searched=s
enior%20internet%20use&page_number=5 (accessed January 31, 2009).

———. 2009. "Less Frequent Internet Users Closing the Gap." http://www.
mediapost.com/publications/index.cfm?fa=Articles.showArticle&art_aid
=98128&passFuseAction=PublicationsSearch.showSearchReslts&art_sear
ched=senior%20internet%20use&page_number=1 (accessed January 14,
2009).

Martin, Steve. 2007. *Born Standing Up*. New York: Simon & Schuster Audio.

Matlack, Carol. 2007. "Chi-Chi Meets Quirky." *BusinessWeek*, September 10, 45.

McGregor, Jena. 2008. "Customer Service Champs." *BusinessWeek*, March 3.

McManus, Chris. 2002. *Right Hand, Left Hand: The Origins of Asymmetry in Brains,
Bodies, Atoms and Cultures*. Cambridge, MA: Harvard University Press.

Nelson, Emily. 2001. "Bottom Line: Diaper Sales Sagging, P & G Thinks Young to
Reposition Pampers." *Wall Street Journal*, December 27, p. A1.

Penn, Mark J. 2007. *Microtrends*. New York: Twelve, Hachette Book Group USA.

Ramsey, Sheila J. 1998. "Interactions between North Americans and Japanese:
Considerations of Communication Style." In *Basic Concepts of Intercultural
Communication*, edited by Michael J. Bennett. Yarmouth, ME: Intercultural Press,
111–30.

Rosenbloom, Stephanie. 2006. "In Certain Circles, Two Is a Crowd." *New York
Times*, November 16, Thursday Styles, p. 1. LexisNexis key word "proxemics"
(accessed January 13, 2009).

Salonen, Esa-Pekka. 2008. "Salon Series," Chicago Symphony Orchestra, January 22.

Serrell, Beverly. 1996. *Museum Labels*. Walnut Creek, CA: AltaMira Press.

Simon, Nina. 2009. "Letting Go of the CEO Superstar." *Museum News*, January–
February, 33–35.

Smith, Perry M. 1998. *Rules and Tools for Leaders.* Garden City Park, NY: Avery Publishing Group.

Snyder, James S., and Joan Darragh. 1993. *Museum Design: Planning and Building for Art.* New York: Oxford University Press.

"Sources of Support for U.S. Museums, FY06 (IMLS Survey)." 2009. *Museum Investor* 1, no. 4 (winter).

Sternin, Jerry. 2009. "The Positive Deviance Initiative Story." http://www.policyinnovations.org/ideas/innovations/data/PositiveDeviance (accessed January 13, 2009).

Storti, Craig. 1999. *Figuring Foreigners Out.* Yarmouth, ME: Intercultural Press, 53–65.

Townsend, Robert B. 2009. "The Status of Women and Minorities in the History Profession." http://www.historians.org/perspectives/Issues/2002/0204/0204pro1.cfm (accessed January 31, 2009).

Underhill, Paco. 1999. *Why We Buy: The Science of Shopping.* New York: Simon & Schuster.

———. 2005. *Call of the Mall.* New York: Simon & Schuster.

Welch, Jack, and Suzy Welch. 2009. "Of Boards and Blame." *BusinessWeek,* January 26–February 2, 102.

Index

About the Author

Margot A. Wallace is an associate professor of marketing communication at Columbia College Chicago. Her publications include *Museum Branding*, the first book to address the brand building aspect of museum marketing. She speaks on arts marketing at conferences throughout the United States and internationally, including talks in Canada, England, the Netherlands, Australia, and Bulgaria.